W9-DAB-308

Is Anybody Listening When I Pray?

Ron & Myrna
Neff

1982

Is Anybody Listening When I Pray?

Phoebe Cranor

Bethany Fellowship INC.
MINNEAPOLIS, MINNESOTA 55438

Scripture quotations before each chapter are taken from *The Jerusalem Bible*, copyright © 1966 by Darton, Longman & Todd, Ltd., and Doubleday & Company, Inc. Used by permission of the publishers.

Copyright © 1980
Phoebe Cranor
All Rights Reserved

Published by Bethany Fellowship, Inc.
6820 Auto Club Road, Minneapolis, Minnesota 55438

Printed in the United States of America

Library of Congress Cataloging in Publication Data

Cranor, Pheobe.
    Is anybody listening when I pray?

        SUMMARY: Twenty essays on various aspects of prayer.
        1. Prayer—Juvenile literature. [1. Prayer]
    I. Title
    BV212.C73   248.3'2   79-27475
    ISBN 0-87123-200-6

Dedication

Wisdom and inspiration don't always come from the adults of this world. Much of my own spiritual development has happened through my association with children and young people. I would like to dedicate this book to some specific ones from whom I have learned much about God and His endless love:

Andy, Fritz, Margaret
Ralph, Fern, Bruce, Roy, Harley
Carl, Patty, Polly, Roger
Mike, Dexter, Burt, Cara, Ruth
Brent, Todd, Lois, Dinan
David, Diedre, Becky, Berta Jo
Lynne, Bruce, Katy, Meg
Martha, Helen, Heide, Eric
Thor, Bruce, Evan, Crag
Mike, Mark, David, Susan
Charlie, Andy
Debra, Brenda, John
Beverly, David, Paul
Madelaine, Lori, Larry, Kim
Russell, Jill, Jess, Jennifer
Judy, Joan, Helen, Nancy, Jackie, Bobby
Doug, Jon, Susan
Alex, Beth, Kathy

About the Author

Phoebe Cranor is the wife of a Colorado cattle rancher and the mother of four children. She has taught in the Arizona public school system and has nineteen years' experience teaching children and young people in Sunday school. Presently she is active in an inner-healing prayer and counseling group.

Mrs. Cranor has a B.A. degree from the Arizona State University. Her stories, poems and articles have appeared in periodicals through the years and she has authored three thought-provoking books: *Why Did God Let Grandpa Die?*, 1976, *Why Doesn't God Do Something?*, 1978, and *How Am I Supposed to Love Myself?*, 1979, Bethany Fellowship, Inc.

Table of Contents

Index of Scripture Passages

Preface

Much of my own spiritual growth has come about through discussions with young people. They are open and usually much more aware than we give them credit for. Their questions are honest. They try desperately to square what they feel with what they hear and see. Sometimes it doesn't fit as well as we all wish it did. Their worries used to worry me. I used to think I had to provide them with logical answers to every question. Now I realize that each human being is at least as loved by God, the Father, as by me. If I so painfully long to help a young person find the truth which will set free, how much more does God yearn after wholeness for all of His children? Now I am finally letting go of my own inadequacies and trusting God's gift of the Holy Spirit to speak to my friends. Sometimes He uses my voice and my writing. Sometimes He steps over them as ineffectual and speaks through His own power. All I know is that I am wiliing to contribute what I have—which I have only because He has given it to me—and let Him do as He sees fit with it. Happily, prayer and love are powerful channels, even when words fail.

My friend Jim, in this book, is a composite of many of the young men and women who have joined my extended family. When I finished writing his year-long journey toward growing up, somehow he had become his own person. His questions, already real on the lips of countless maturing young people, lived even more dramatically in my own life, and the answers to them affected me, too. Perhaps Jim will become a spokesman for the youth in other lives. Perhaps teachers and parents will identify not only with Jim as a person, but with my efforts to speak to him and his friends. Maybe whoever uses this book in a classroom or at home, perhaps reading it together with the young adults in his charge, will ask the Holy Spirit to speak through it and above it to needs and longings of the human spirit. There is a bit of Jim's search going on, still, in every grown-up. In fact, some of his questions were my own only a few years ago.

Many of us have never even glimpsed the width and depth of God's love for His children. The world is aching and destroying itself because the picture has never gotten to it that a loving Father created it out of love and for love. He has given us the choice, just as He did the first man and woman in the Garden, to live in daily communion with that Love or to go our own way without it. The present human dilemma is the direct result of our choice, collectively and individually. If we, who have even an hour a week to deal with our young people, can somehow become channels for God's love to them, we can do a great deal to alter world conditions. Love is more powerful than evil. Enough love, such as that which Jesus showed us when He died for our sins, will cancel out even death. He proved it. He did it for us, even while we were still sinners. Then He commanded us to go out into all the world and show forth the Good News. Let's give our fear of unknowns away to the Holy Spirit and confront the evil head-on by speaking out to the future generation about God's love. If we open up the smallest channels of our own willingness, He will pour through that which He is longing to give each one of us.

Is Anybody Listening When I Pray?

Everyone moved by the Spirit is a son of God. The spirit you received is not the spirit of slaves bringing fear into your lives again; it is the spirit of sons, and it makes us cry out, "Abba, Father!"—Romans 8:14-15

Chapter 1

"Prayer Is for the Birds!"

What is prayer?

"Prayer is for the birds!"

Jim, the school friend of my children, was sitting beside me in the car. I looked at him in surprise.

"You didn't like it when we said grace at dinner?"

He shook his head emphatically. "That's not what I meant. Grace is okay. I mean *praying!*"

Jim had ridden to our ranch with my children on the school bus and I was taking him home. We were having a short time together in the car; but I was not in the least prepared for his out-of-the-blue comment.

"Tell me what you meant when you said 'praying,' Jim." I was glad we lived far enough from town that we'd have a few minutes to talk. Jim and his family were regulars in church. He was speaking about something he knew—or at least had strong feelings about.

"Well . . ." The boy clasped his hands tightly in his lap. I held my breath.

"When the pastor looks up at the rafters and starts sing-songing along through his nose, it gives me a dip."

"A dip?"

"Yeah. A down."

"Oh, you mean it makes you depressed. Do you ever listen to what he prays about?"

"Sometimes. He prays about all-right stuff. But it's a waste of time. I think he just fills up a certain amount of time between other things like the sermon and the collection."

"What don't you like about the prayers? Why are they depressing to you?"

Jim shrugged his shoulders.

"What would you like to have instead?"

"I like singing; or the organ. I even like just nothing—quiet, sort of."

"If prayer from the pulpit bothers you, what about other kinds of prayer?"

Jim thought awhile. Finally he shook his head.

"I guess," he said quietly, "that I just stop listening when somebody starts praying."

"That makes sense. We do it all the time—shut out what we've decided we don't want to hear."

We were nearly to Jim's house and I desperately wanted to pursue the matter with him. "Would you listen to me if I told you some of the things I have found out about prayer? Would you meet me again to talk about it?"

You never know about young people. My offer might have frightened him away from the matter of prayer for years. I waited in silence. Finally he gave me a little sideways look and ducked his head.

"I'd like it. Will you bake chocolate chip cookies like I had at your house last week?"

I laughed. Maybe my cookies had more drawing power than my lectures, but I was game to try to uncover a new spot in Jim's spiritual growth by any means available. "It's a deal."

He got out and I drove home, pondering the beauty of my moment: the gift of this young man putting his hand in mine to walk into a new path with the Lord.

A few days later over a large plate of chocolate chip cookies and mugs of milk, Jim did listen to me as I talked about prayer. He cared. It was a miracle right in the midst of television cowboys and cartoon heroes and the after-school gang. I moved with caution and a great deal of silent prayer of my own.

FOR JIM:

Every now and then, I think, words get in the way of ideas. We hear a certain word and a picture immediately comes into our minds. Sometimes the picture stops us from thinking about what the word really means. The word we were talking about earlier was "prayer." Lots of times we think certain things about prayer that aren't included in what it means at all.

Suppose you knew a man who was smart and wise and rich. Besides that, he was generous and interesting and fun. Suppose he had all the time in the world for you; you were sure he loved you best of all. And *then* let's suppose that he was your very own father with whom you lived all the time.

How would you act with a father like that? You'd tell him everything that happened to you, either good or bad. You'd share your fun. You'd ask him to help every time you got into a jam. You'd discuss your friends with him. You'd make him nice presents and tell him how great you thought he was. And you'd be absolutely positive that he would take care of whatever you needed for your own good.

Well, we do have a Father like that. He is our heavenly Father, God. He is all the things we described in our "suppose" and more besides; and when we tell Him everything that happens, good and bad, share our fun and our problems and our friends, when we tell Him we love Him, we are praying. That is what prayer is.

The point of prayer is not what we say or how we say it; the point is *to whom we say it*. Prayer is based on the relationship we have with a living, caring Person. The first step toward learning about prayer is seeing that we are talking to Someone who is listening and acting on what He hears.

If you had a father who was unkind and cruel and didn't care about you at all, you would not talk to him as much or as happily—maybe you wouldn't talk to him at all—as you would to a good, kind, loving father. The reason is obvious: you would not have faith in him. You wouldn't know for sure that he'd listen without laughing or betraying you, or that he would help you instead of hurting you. A relationship that makes you want to pray is based on love and trust in the Person you are talking to. You would then know from experience that He cares and will help you.

The kind of prayer that we were discussing just now is a personal, private conversation with a loving Person. Suppose, though, that you had to talk to that Person in a big room full of people, all listening to you. That is what the minister or priest is doing when he prays in church. He doesn't speak to God the same as he might if he were alone with his Father. Some of the people in his congregation may not know the Father the way he does, so they are listening to his prayers without taking into consideration the loving Person he is addressing. Wouldn't it be hard to talk over important things with someone if you had a whole room full of people listening? So some prayers do sound strange to you just because everyone else is listening to them. God is hearing, too, though, which makes it all right.

Another confusing matter is this: people often pray using "thee" and "thine" and such words when they talk to God. The reason is that a long time ago when the King James Version of the Bible was made, it was translated into the language the people were using. If you had been living then, you really would have said to your mother, "Mother, I pray thee, wilt thou give me a cookie?" It sounds very odd to us, but people talked that way to each other in everyday life. We no longer do. However, the King James Bible still has that kind of language in it. It sounds reverent and loving, and many people have grown up with it so they go on using it when they talk to God. To many of us it sounds stilted. When we don't talk Old English to anyone *but* God, we sometimes get the idea that talking to God has to be different and strange. It really doesn't have to. God can understand any language. When we know Him and love Him, we can speak whatever way we like and be sure He is understanding.

I can understand how you feel about prayer in church. Still, there is a good reason why it is an important part of the service. When a lot of people unite in praying for one certain thing, it is a powerful force for good. We don't know how, but we do know that when a group of people pray for good, lots of good happens.

The first step in understanding prayer in church is for you to pray in private. We may talk with our heavenly Father any time we want to if we have been born into God's family. If you have turned away from sin and asked God's Son to be your Savior, Jim, I'm going to make a suggestion to you: whenever you are in church and prayer time comes, listen to see what your minister is praying about and then join him, saying in your own words whatever you think your rich, loving Father needs to hear from you, His child Jim.

You'll see, if you watch, that He is doing something special about each prayer, at least inside of you. Sometimes you find out later how He answered. Sometimes you only feel, deep inside, that He has, even though you don't know how.

*"And whoever comes to me I shall not turn him away.
And anybody who loves me will be loved by my Father, and
I shall love him and show myself to him."—John 6:37
and 14:21*

Chapter 2

"What If?" Games

How can I be sure someone is listening?

After the first session about prayer, I knew that Jim
would be back. He had truly listened, cookies notwithstanding, and afterward had been unusually quiet and
thoughtful. We set up another meeting in the park after
school.

"Yes," I promised, "I will bring a treat." I could feel
that this young person was actively reaching, growing, and
in tune with his deepest needs as few adults are. I felt the
drawing power of truth, too, along with him. Still I was surprised when the phone rang two days before our "date."

"Tell me something," Jim said tensely. "How can I *be
sure* that somebody who cares is listening to me when I
pray? I tried it, but I couldn't be sure He was there." I
sensed *emergency* in his every inflection. Just because a
person is young doesn't mean he can't have deep troubles.

"Do you want to meet today instead of day after tomorrow?" I asked him. "I have to get some groceries. I could
stop over—"

"Not at my house."

I could hear his plea coming through loud and clear.

"No, I think the park would suit me better," I finished

quickly. We arranged a meeting and I scooped up a bag of goodies to take along—and a sweater, for the weather was getting cold.

Jim sat hunched at a park table. I could see immediately that he had a bad problem. He didn't waste any time.

"My dad lost his job and my mom is sick with something that might really be bad. I'm worried. I don't know what is going to happen. If prayer is for real, I'll pray—what else can I do?"

I knew that no platitudes would suffice for Jim. This was a moment to avoid pat answers and pious mouthings and get to the heart of the matter. What else *could* he do? And if he prayed and nothing happened? Well, Lord, I believe; help my unbelief. Putting my bag on the table, I sat down across from him.

FOR JIM:

Jim, nobody can do much about big problems like yours. The main reason you are worried is that you don't know what the future holds. What a person does when he can't figure out the future is play all kinds of "what if?" games:

"What if my father doesn't find another job and we run clear out of money?"

"What if my mother has to go to the hospital and have an operation? What if, in fact, she dies?"

We can't ever know the answers to "what if?" questions. They will drive us crazy if we let them, with all the terrible possibilities we can think of.

So I am going to suggest an entirely different approach. You told me on the phone that you didn't feel sure there was anybody hearing you when you prayed. There is a way to do something about that. Maybe the first thing we need to do is take care of the "who hears?" part of your problem.

God spoke to His people over and over again. The Old Testament of the Bible tells us how He spoke to the people in one way and then another. He used circumstances and He used individuals. Sometimes He used angels and one time He even used a donkey. Sometimes the people heard Him and sometimes they didn't. The prophets often complained because they heard what God was telling them very clearly but nobody else would pay any attention when they spoke about it. Finally, after several thousand years, God sent Jesus to earth. A man among men, while still being God, He spoke to people in their own language. He could speak to them in ways they understood because He had become one of them.

Jesus had a purpose in His life. It was to show and demonstrate the nature of God: His love and caring, His forgiveness, His complete power over all wickedness, even death. After Jesus' short life on earth was over, He sent the Holy Spirit to go on teaching us—everybody, everywhere, ever since—what God is like. That is the best news we have, because through the power of our Friend, the Holy Spirit, we can meet Jesus in person just as well as the people did when He lived here. Of course that is a mystery. We can't actually see Him, at least not the way I am seeing you right now. But, believe it or not, when we invite Him to come and be with us, not just on the outside but *inside* us, He will do it. He will accept our invitation and, as some say, "come into our hearts."

All that expression means is that both inside and outside we are aware of His presence. You yourself know how that is. Sometimes you are very much aware that somebody is near you, even though you are not looking at that individual at all. And sometimes you know so well what a person close to you is feeling that you can say you are almost inside that person. When Jesus comes into our lives, He is both nearby, as a Friend standing outside your skin but close; and He is also inside as one you know very, very well. Both your mind and your feelings respond to Him.

When we ask Jesus to come into our lives, and He does, we will know it. Some people are aware of His presence in one way and some in another. Some know it instantly; some know it in a few days. But everyone who really asks for Jesus will find that He has made himself known in that person's life. He will find that the hard things he was worried about are still there, but they are different. They don't bother him so much. He has what Jesus promised: peace in a deep spot inside that makes the "what if?" questions not so terrible. "After all," one says to himself, "nothing can happen that Jesus and I can't handle." His being there takes away the pressure of worry.

Some people invite Jesus into the living room and try to keep Him out of the rest of the house. But He wants us to ask Him into room after room until there is no part of the house in which He doesn't belong. Some people ask Him in and then leave Him sitting, never stopping to get acquainted with Him, too. They ask Him into their lives when the going is tough and then sort of forget about Him as soon as things ease up a bit.

The best way, though, is to start by saying, "Jesus, I want you to come into my heart and show me what God's love is like in my own life. I have sinned against you, and I want to stop. Please help me." Then you can begin to get acquainted with Him just as you do any other good person you've met. You can read about Him (in the Bible), talk to Him (in prayer), and talk with other people about Him (in testimony). All three of those things help you to handle the problems you are bound to have in your life—like your father losing his job and your mother getting sick.

Jesus doesn't want people to be sick or hurting. He will touch them and heal them wherever they hurt worst. He won't do magic tricks, though, and fix everything up just the way you want Him to. He knows what you need for the best in your whole life. Even though it is hard to understand at the time, something like losing a job can be the very best thing that happens to a person. Maybe there is a much better job waiting for your father. Maybe as your mother gets well she will learn a new kind of love direct from God that will make her life much better. You just can't tell.

What you *can* do is ask Jesus to make himself known to you and then see what happens next. Will you try it? Don't plan what will happen. Just tell Him that you want Him to be your friend, come into your heart, and forgive your sins and mistakes. Then see how He manages to show you that He did it. He will. He always does.

*As tenderly as a father treats his children, so Yahweh
treats those who fear him; . . . Yahweh has fixed his throne
in the heavens, his empire is over all. Bless Yahweh, all
his angels, heroes mighty to enforce his word, attentive to his
word of command.— Psalm 103:13, 19-20*

Chapter 3

The Executive

How can God hear everyone at once?

I went home from our meeting with my heart in my
throat. Jim was so tender and vulnerable. Supposing he
would be hurt by the other young people who failed to understand or care what happened to him. I was sure, I guess,
that our Lord Jesus would touch him and he'd know it. But
somewhere after that security, my faith wavered. I *know*
life is hard. Of course I also know that Jesus in one's heart is
adequate protection from the hurts which are an inevitable
part of being human. I caught myself playing the same
"what if?" game I had warned Jim against. Yes, "what if?"
is a sneaky little voice which gets itself into our minds at
the slightest provocation.

"Lord," I prayed, "I know you *can* do everything that I
can see needs doing, and then some. You know the big picture. I deliberately make the effort to turn all this over to
you." Immediately I experienced a great peace. I am not
stuck with the job of making things work out. That is God's
work. All I have to do is be the witness who tells what I
know from experience—what has happened to me. I know
that when I asked Him to come into my life, Jesus Christ,
Son of God, the Savior, did. I know that He does it for ev-

eryone else who asks Him; that is all I have to say to Jim. The rest is up to Him.

I put away my groceries, excited and a little bit trembly, thinking with anticipation of what Jim's and my next meeting would be like. I knew well the fascinating path he would be stepping into, somewhere new all the time, if Jim truly asked for the Savior to be in his life. Would he? And when Jesus responded to Jim's request, would Jim acknowledge it and move with it?

I needn't have worried a bit about Jim. He asked; and Jesus, true to His promise, "Ask and you will receive," responded. Jim was wide-eyed with the newness of his personal meeting with Jesus Christ, Son of God.

"All by myself," he told me in awe. "I was just all by myself and there—there He *was*." I didn't need to ask him, "How did you know?" There was no doubt he had experienced mentally, emotionally, physically and spiritually the presence truly with him.

As far as questions, though, Jim's meeting with Jesus had raised more than it had answered. They poured out of him so fast I had to stop him.

"Take it easy, Pal. I can't answer so many questions, especially all at once. Let's pick out the one you think is most important and leave the rest until next time." Jim sat in silence, munching his roll, for a long, thoughtful moment.

"Well," he said, finally, "I guess that now I've met Him the way I have, I don't see how He can hear me and everybody else at the same time. Even if God and Jesus and the Holy Spirit are three as well as just One, there are still about a trillion people talking at the same time—some even in other languages. How can He hear and manage to do anything about all those things?"

"And run the solar system and enforce the law of gravity, not to mention looking after every sparrow like it says in the Bible," I added. Jim laughed, but his look was puzzled.

"Yeah. How can He?"

I recognized this particular question as having come along with the personal relationship that Jim's recent experience with the living Lord had begun. It was a question I had heard from people of all ages, from my kindergarteners to adults. The reality of the person of Jesus changes all our old ideas of God and His caring. Instead of an idea or a philosophy, He suddenly becomes extremely personal. We lose track of the power and magnificence, the awe-inspiring magnitude of God, Creator and King of His universe. I am not sure I can keep both of those concepts on an equal balance in my own mind. How could I expect a young person to do so? Yet, if he is to pray truly and his prayer have meaning, the question must be resolved. Nobody will pray very long to somebody he suspects has His mind on something else.

"All right, Lord. I'm going to make a try at it. Please put your words in my mouth."

FOR JIM:

Sometimes on television we see a big executive at work. We see him with several telephones and secretaries. He is talking into one telephone and, at the same time, signing a paper. Another phone is ringing and another secretary is ready with something else for him to sign while he talks. This is maybe an exaggerated picture of what happens in the life of a person who has a big, important business which he knows how to handle very well. You know the feeling of doing several things at once. I know you can eat a snack, listen to a tape, do your homework and pet the dog with your foot—maybe even keep watch on the clock, too, all at the same time. But that's about where it ends. If you are doing a very hard math problem while you are eating and listening to a tape and petting the dog, maybe you'll stop hearing the words of the song and forget to take a bite, just because you are concentrating so hard on the math.

Somewhere inside of us, no matter what we *say* we believe about God, most of us have a picture that says God is really like a regular person. If He is like a person, we feel, then He can do only so much and no more. That is the logical way to feel because we know ourselves and we know that we are limited in what we can do.

But God is much more than a person. He has a force, a power, which flows through the entire universe, keeping the solar system (and who knows how many others there are besides our own) in order, controlling the instincts of animals, making the atoms and the grains of sand and everything else operate. God couldn't be like one person. He has to be a whole lot more. He has to be able to do not just what one of us could do, but whatever needs doing in the whole universe. Think of the force of His intelligence as love, which is what Jesus called it; and think of it as flowing over and under and through everything that has been created—then you can see that God isn't like even the big executive who can run a huge company but who eventually runs out of time and energy to take care of everything.

Praying to God isn't like talking to some big super computer, either. When Jesus came to earth, He told us that God is like a loving father whom the tiny child calls "Da-da." What Jesus meant was that, besides having the force of His intelligence going through the universe and the big love that created it keeping it going, God *cares* about everything like a loving father does. The concept is a mystery that nobody can understand. How could He, we wonder, really care about everything at once? There is no way to answer that question. Well, yes, there is a way. We can try Him out. If we can get rid of the idea of a big-executive God who can do only so much and no more, then we can go back to praying to Someone who is as interested in you as He would be if He had only five children. He knows your feelings, your needs, your hopes, your troubles, as well as all the good things He put into you.

Do you realize that you are the only person ever since time began who is exactly like you? God worked it out so there would never be two people just alike. So you are the only one who prays to Him the way you do. You are safe to put your life in His hands because He made you unique— the only one. He made you to be His friend. Nothing is better than that. He has lots of friends and He cares for each one just as much as the rest. He knows what is best for them all, too, which is more than I can say for anybody else.

Ever since God created the world his everlasting power and deity—however invisible—have been there for the mind to see in the things he has made.—Romans 1:20

Chapter 4

The Shipwreck

How can I know there is a God?

"I guess prayer won't work, after all."

Jim was obviously downcast. I know how rough the road is for a beginner on any path, so I wasn't surprised that he had met with a pitfall. I was a little taken back by what it was, though. Jim was young, bright and tuned in, but still not yet very mature. The question he was pondering must have come from somebody else.

Sure enough, it finally came out.

"Well, my uncle says that it's a stupid joke to pray. He says people have just made up God to fit their own needs. How can we pray to someone we've made up in the first place?"

Jim had had a personal encounter with the living Lord. How could he ask that question? I knew how. The blasé older man-of-the-world cynic, representing authority and wisdom and worldliness, had spoken. Jim's idolized uncle could overrule the childlike love and simplicity of this boy's new-found faith with a flash of his superior wit. Well, he could if there weren't Someone else with stronger wit. "Lord, please, *please* give me something so convincing that this new disciple will hear it over the sound of his disdainful uncle's voice. You did that for me long ago, Lord, when an important figure in my life fed me that same illogical logic."

"Keep going back," I heard an inner voice saying. "Go back behind the beginning of the argument." Behind the beginning? "Lord, why do you speak in riddles?"

But it wasn't a riddle. As I started to talk to Jim, I heard my voice doing exactly as I had been told. I went back behind the beginning. And as I spoke, my old inner doubts swept before me and disappeared into the joy of the new touch of my Master's presence. Never does one person come to a new happiness in the Lord without bringing along someone else.

FOR JIM:

Suppose you were, let's say, shipwrecked alone on a desert island. Suppose, in the course of the shipwreck, you had a bump on the head that made you forget the names of things. You could walk around and do all you were used to doing, but you just couldn't remember what to call the objects about you.

Suppose the first thing you did was to fall down into a dark hole, and a pile of big leaves fell in on top of you. The dust from the leaves filled your lungs and made you cough. You gasped for air and struggled to the side of the hole and up out of it as fast as you could to get to the air and breathe again. You needed air, whether you could remember its name or not. And you tried to find it with all your might. This is called an instinct.

We have a lot of instincts. They aren't thought out. Instead, they are inside us and push us to get whatever it is we need. If you were still on that desert island, you would become thirsty almost at once. You might not know the name of water, but you would go looking for it; and as soon as you found it, you would drink some. Then you would find something to eat and hurry up to eat it. Probably if you were on a desert island, you wouldn't know the names of the berries, even if you didn't get a bump on the head. But your instinct would make you put them in your mouth because you were hungry. If the things you ate and drank were poisonous, you would be sick. That wouldn't be because food and water in general weren't what you needed. It would be only because some *particular* kind of food or water wasn't good for you.

It wouldn't do us much good to spend a lot of time wondering why we have the instincts to find air and water and food. We have them just the same way we have joints in our knees and our fingers and hair on our heads. That is the way we were made. It is part of us. Some people have stronger instincts than others. Some people also have stronger arms and are taller and smarter than others, too. Still, most people have some height and strength and intelligence and instincts that are just part of being human.

There is another desire everyone has that is like an instinct, in a way. It is a need to be loved. Neither babies' bodies nor their intelligence develop properly unless they have a certain amount of love. Love is not a thing we can see, like food and water. It isn't even exactly like air, since scientists have found what goes into air and can take it apart to make gasses. Just the same, love is real. One of the proofs that it is real is that people die without it. Somehow or other we all came up with a need for love, along with the other characteristics that make us people.

Does anybody think our needs for food and water, air, warmth, and love are made up? It doesn't seem likely since tiny babies all have those needs and the instincts to try to get them just as soon as they are born. Whoever made us in the first place must have put all those instincts in us, along with the shape of us and our general characteristics.

Now we'll get to the question about people making up the idea of God to fit their needs. All through history we find people everywhere worshipping God. As far back as we have any evidence of human life, we have evidence of some sort of worship. People show by their actions that there is one more thing they need—and they have an instinct to try to find it. They have a need to worship God—somebody outside themselves who is greater than they are. If people made up God, where did they get the idea that they needed God? Whoever made them in the first place must have put that in them, along with eyes, hands, feet, and mouths. So even if people evolved God to fit their needs, they only would be going along with what He made them need.

Besides having the instincts, we also have things here on this earth to satisfy every instinct. We need air, we want air, and air is here for us. We need and want food, and food is here. We need and want water, and it is here, too. Love is here to meet our need for it. All of our needs are built into us by our Maker, who made not only the needs but also put something on the earth to fill every one of them. Does it seem logical that there would be one longing inside of every person, since people first began, that would have *nothing* here to satisfy it? If everyone has always desired God, He must have made us want Him because He knew it was a good idea—and because He is there to satisfy the longing.

As we study religion from the beginning of history, we find that the need for love and the need for God have gradually come together; so we know, now, that we can have both love and God at the same time. Jesus taught us that. Before He came along, there was a great deal of worship without the people understanding love—or at least, without understanding how it came from God. The last two thousand years, since Jesus came, we have had the picture of God that He gave us: total and complete love as shown by Jesus. We can see how our instincts for love and for worship have finally come together in Him.

There is one more answer to your question about God. Dreams are real, aren't they? You have them and I have them. So does everybody else. Even people who think they don't dream are just forgetting their dreams before they wake up; scientists have proven that when our sleep is disturbed so we can't dream, we get sick and, I suppose, would eventually die. When you tell me your dreams, there is no way you can prove to me that what you say you dreamed is what you *did* dream. All you can do is tell me and leave it up to me whether or not to believe you.

Still, whether or not I believe you does not in any way change what you dreamed. It is just as real if I don't believe you as if I do. Your dream is part of your own unique experience.

Whenever a person is ready to meet Jesus personally, Jesus will come to him in a very real, personal way, just as He did to you. That is in no way altered by having someone else tell you it didn't happen. Just as your dream was a real part of your life, no matter who knows about it, so the presence of Jesus in your heart is real.

What happened to you, Jim, is called "Experiencing His Presence." A person who has not yet had that kind of personal experience with Jesus may tell you it isn't true, but it will not have any effect on the truth. It didn't happen to that person; it happened to *you*. Of course it has happened to millions of people since Jesus came to earth, so it wasn't *just* you. You can continue to pray to the person who came to you because you have experienced His reality. It is too bad that your uncle hasn't invited Him into his life yet; but it isn't your problem. You have had the experience and you know Jesus, so you can pray to Him and know for sure that He hears, loves, and stays with you.

Is there a man among you who would hand his son a stone when he asked for bread? Or would hand him a snake when he asked for a fish? If you, then, who are evil, know how to give your children what is good, how much more will your Father in heaven give good things to those who ask him!—Matthew 7:9-12

Chapter 5

The Fairy Tale

Why doesn't God always answer my prayers?

"What do you think will happen?" Jim seemed worried. He took all of his questions so seriously that I often had to kid around with him a bit to help him with his balance. Life isn't always dead serious with the Lord.

"What do you think will happen next week, because half the people are praying for a snowstorm so there'll be skiing, and the rest are praying for nice weather so their friends won't get stranded when they drive in for Homecoming? If God answers some of their prayers, then He can't possibly answer the rest."

"Do you think 'answering' always means giving what somebody wants?"

"Well, yes, I s'pose I do."

"What would your mother say if you asked her to give you a thousand dollars?"

"She'd say 'no!' That's one thing sure."

"Maybe God will have to say 'no' to some of the people who are praying for a certain kind of weather this weekend."

I thought about what I had just said to Jim. "No" is so

hard to accept. In our lives many things are instant and easy. Permissiveness is the order of the day. Long-range goods are often forgotten in our search for the momentary satisfactions. We feel compelled to tell ourselves as well as our children that everything, no matter how hard it really is, is "fun." Discipline and delayed satisfaction play a much less imporant role in our lives than they did in days gone by. At least, that is the way it looks to me. So how does our relationship to God fit into the trend of the times? Often, I fear, we treat Him like some sort of "instant cash card" with which, if we know how, we can get whatever it is we want. Even if our wants are other-centered, like peace and freedom, we often ask God to do it for us without making any sort of disciplined sacrifice to help it happen.

Real deep relationship, though, is another matter altogether. I will work my own life to its limit for a relationship I treasure. I will willingly, without even thinking about it, discipline and sacrifice for someone I love more than anything else. His ideas and goals will become my own. Relationship with God is something entirely different from the want-get-have of a self-centered perspective. How in the world can I help Jim see that a God from whom we only get is bound to be dethroned eventually?

FOR JIM:

Fairy stories are always full of magic. We daydream about Aladdin's lamp that gives us our wishes. The idea of being able to get our wish has always appealed very much to us. So lots of people think of God as some kind of super magician who will give us our wishes if we do and say exactly the right things. They work hard at getting the right formula in mind and the right techniques for prayer so the magic will work. After a while they realize it isn't working and then, sometimes, they get unhappy with God and disillusioned with prayer.

"I prayed and prayed for something," they say, "and nothing happened. I guess prayer just doesn't work." Then somebody else tells a story about a person who prayed for something and that very thing happened almost at once. There's even a song about a little girl praying for scarlet ribbons for her hair and getting them. It leaves us a bit confused.

To see if we can get at the bottom of the confusion, let's pretend that the get-exactly-what-you-want kind of prayer really happens. You ask for a bicycle and for a friend and for straight teeth and for an A on your paper. You ask for your team to win the softball game. You ask that your house be painted and the garbage be taken out. Everything you can think of that you want, you can pray for and immediately receive.

It is all great sport for a while—until you run out of ideas. You can ask for more and more things and get them until nothing is any fun at all. You win without trying and get good grades without studying. You can do sports without practicing. Kids like you without your having to work at being nice. After a while you begin to see that you can't earn anything, or be paid, or be proud of yourself for what you have done. You can't take any credit for anything and you can't feel good about anything you are doing. What is life all about if there is nothing to do but ask for exactly what you want and then get it?

By now you can see that a God-is-magic would not be the kind of God who would be your friend, sharing work and play and hurts and joyful surprises with you. He would be just a giant machine like the gum ball dispensers in the front of the supermarket. After a short time of exploring the newness of Him, you would be bored and give Him up for something else.

Jesus showed us that life has a purpose, life is going somewhere. Everything we do and say and think and feel is part of a much larger whole which He called "eternity." God is love and we are here to learn as much about love as we can. If God were to start being a magic wand for us and giving us things all the time, we would most likely overlook the purpose of our being here. Our natural selfishness would take over and we would miss out on all the experiences which teach us about love. God is, as we said before, a wonderful Friend who loves each one of us. Friendship is much better than all of our wishes being granted. Friendship means growing and becoming all we were created to become. You have all sorts of surprises inside you that you haven't even thought of. That is called your "potential." As soon as you meet and become acquainted with your heavenly Father, you begin finding out about those surprises and making use of them.

How do you pray, then? How do you talk to Someone who loves you and knows you and wants the very best for you? You tell Him exactly how you feel. You tell Him what you want and the way you think things ought to be. But then, instead of expecting Him to fix them up just the way you say, you tell Him that you realize He knows more about you and everybody else than you do and, in spite of what you want at the moment, you are willing to turn everything over to Him. You give Him your permission to do what is best for you and those you love. Then you wait and watch to see what wonderful ideas He has for you. That frees you of the need to plan everything for yourself.

Speaking of planning: if you had to pray for just your

own needs and could decide exactly what was to happen, that would be hard enough. But suppose you wanted to pray for, say, your father. Wouldn't it be a worry to try to figure out what to ask for in *his* life? If you knew that precisely what you prayed for were going to happen, it would be such a big responsibility that you would worry yourself sick trying to decide what to ask for. It is so much better to know and trust a loving, all-wise God to whom you can turn over everything and be sure He will take the right kind of care of it.

A God who is your friend at all times is a great deal more exciting than a magician who has a whole bag full of tricks to dole out. Learning about love is, in fact, the most exciting thing in the world. You feel good every time you realize you have a new idea about the nature of love. When that happens, you can laugh with your heavenly Father about a new step in eternity!

A man is trapped when he shouts "Dedicated!" and only begins to reflect after the vow.—Proverbs 20:25

Chapter 6

The Bargain

Is God more likely to hear me if I promise Him something?

"My dad hasn't got a job yet, and he's afraid because he doesn't know how to pay for Mom's hospital bills." Jim's eyes were heavy with worry. His compassion for the pain of his parents touched me. It wasn't himself he was most worried about (although his own fear showed very clearly). He was experiencing the helplessness we all feel when those we love are struggling.

What can I say to him? I wondered. I have no pat answers. My own life is full of the goodness of God in the midst of my worst problems. But it is *my* life. Jim must find his own experiences. Jim's voice was going on, quietly determined.

"So I think I'll tell God that if He will find my dad a job, I'll go to school and be a minister. He would like that, wouldn't He?"

Dear Lord, I thought, this young man is so intense and so caring. If he bargains with you like that, he will spend the rest of his life carrying out his part of the bargain—even if it is not in your will for him. I took a deep breath. Spontaneous debate is not my talent. Lord, *you* talk to Jim. Here is my voice. He must see that a bargain with you is not the answer to his need.

FOR JIM:

Suppose you had a friend who had something you felt you absolutely had to own. You asked him for it, but he didn't give it to you. You asked two or three times. You felt you just must have it. In a thoughtless moment, you said to him, "I will give you all the money I earn above what I need to live on for the next twenty years if you'll give me what I want."

Your friend could hardly turn down such a good offer so his answer is, "Okay, let's write it up like a contract." You do that and happily take off for your house with whatever it was you wanted so badly.

You enjoy your new possession a lot. For a long time you're happy you have it. It doesn't bother you that you have to pay your friend everything you earn for the next twenty years. But finally, one day, you see something in a store window that you want even more than the first thing. But it costs a lot of money, much more than you have.

Then the feeling hits you that you wish you could save up just a little bit of extra money to get this new possession. Every month you think of that neat thing you could buy if you had some money. You look at the item you bargained for and wonder if you couldn't have managed without it. You look in the store window and wonder if your friend didn't take advantage of you. You get angrier and angrier. Still, you know that you promised on your word of honor to pay him. You even wrote it down and signed your name. Finally you sit down and face the fact that you wish you had never made the bargain at all. You don't even like your friend anymore, but you can't do the things you would like to do because of what you promised him. It was a bad deal.

Now God wouldn't ever take advantage of you like that

pretend "friend" did. But when an honorable person makes a bargain of any kind, he feels that he must keep his promise. This is especially true if the other person has kept his part of the agreement. If you make a deal with God to find your father a job, and your father does locate work, you will feel that you must do what you said you would. That is not the way God operates. He will take care of your father His own way—anyhow. If He listened to bargains, then you would quite possibly come to hate Him because of them.

Many people try to make bargains with God. All it causes is trouble inside themselves. God is not a person who has to be paid to do what you want done or give you what you wish for. He is the God of love who created you and wants you to have the best and be the best that you possibly can achieve. He wants to give you exactly what you need.

It's a good thing God doesn't *ever* let you make a bargain with Him. Let me tell you why. Suppose there were something you wanted very much and you persuaded God to do it; and it was, it turned out, very bad for you. What kind of a father would it be who would give you something that would hurt you just because you wanted it? You would never be able to trust him. Sometimes things happen to us that are not pleasant for us. God makes those events turn out for good, just the same. But if you could make deals with God and they turned out badly—and then you had to spend your whole life "paying" for them, you would become more and more angry and unhappy. Or, in case you decided not to "pay," then you would feel guilty to think you had promised God something and then not kept your promise.

A much better plan, instead of making a deal with God, is to tell Him that you really *do* want to be whatever He wants you to be; He has created your talents and abilities to help you achieve this. Tell Him that you will wait until you are older before you decide whether or not to become a minister. God wants our promise to love, serve and obey Him whether or not He answers our prayers as we think He ought to. Then tell Him just exactly how you feel—how much you care about the problems of your parents and that you are having a hard time trusting Him while you wait for Him to solve them. He understands that you can't see, as He can, what the whole picture looks like. He understands how hard it is to trust Him when you can't see. He is listening.

Let's imagine that we are wrapping all of your worries in a big brown paper package and tying them with a string. Now let's imagine we are handing the package into the hands of Jesus, who takes it and puts it carefully in His pocket. Your parents' problems are now safe with Jesus and, no matter how or when, you can be sure He is taking care of them. Our little pretend is called "using your creative imagination." It is a very good way to pray when you don't know what you need but you know you need *something* very badly. Praying that way is much safer than trying to bribe God with your future.

Be fearless, then, be confident, for go where you will,
Yahweh your God is with you.—Joshua 1:9

Chapter 7

The Backpackers

How does a person "pray without ceasing"?

It was exciting to watch Jim's growth in his spiritual journey. No longer did we have to set up special times for talk about prayer. Whenever we saw each other, we could begin, continue or finish a discussion. He was full of ideas, eager to know more. His was still natural, untainted curiosity and sometimes doubt when things looked illogical or impossible.

One day we had gone skating on a pond together on a cold winter afternoon. A nice big fire on the shore was perfect for a wiener roast. Jim's two little sisters were bounding around, causing him some embarrassment, and our children were giggling over their hot dogs. Out of the blue he said, "What does it mean, 'Pray without ceasing'?" He sat quietly for a moment then continued thoughtfully. "I don't see how I could do that. How'd I ever get my homework done or anything? How'd I ever have any fun? Or eat or sleep? Does anybody *really* pay attention to that verse in the Bible: 'Pray without ceasing'?"

I looked at Jim, his nose red from the cold, and I laughed.

"You sure do ask hard questions sometimes, Jim. And I've asked that one myself a good many times. I'm not even sure I know the answer—the real answer. I know only what I have decided myself. Will that do?" He nodded, his mouth full. Silently I prayed that I could articulate what to me was still only a feeling—an intuition—about how to pray constantly (and still get my work done and have a bit of fun along the way).

FOR JIM:

Supposing you had a great buddy, the best friend anyone could want. The two of you liked to do just about everything together and had to be called apart when your parents wanted you to work at home. One day you got permission from both sets of parents to go on a two-day backpacking trip up the mountain behind your ranch. How carefully you made lists and planned what you would take that would last the two days, keep you comfortable, and could still be carried by the two of you from the start: dried foods and lightweight bedrolls, matches in tight containers, and, don't forget a good map. Finally you got everything together and packed and started off up the trail.

At first you would talk a mile a minute about all sorts of things. You would laugh and joke and be serious, too. It would be such fun to be together with no one to interrupt. But after lunch, maybe, when you were hiking hard uphill, you'd fall silent. It would take most of your breath to get up the mountain and a lot of concentration to keep from falling over the big boulders. Later you'd eat your supper and talk again for a while before you got too sleepy for any more conversation.

The next day would be the same. Sometimes you'd talk a lot and other times you'd walk along silently. You might separate a little way to get around a big rock, although you'd never be out of sight of one another. In the sleeping bags at night you'd be too tired to talk. If you woke up in the night, you'd hear your friend's breath coming and going evenly as he slept beside you. Once, maybe, you'd hear a strange sound and wake him up to help you decide what to do. It would be a wonderful, companionable trip. You'd talk about your future and important matters and you'd tease and joke. You'd do things, make decisions and rest.

There would be one consistent point about your trip together, though. That would be the fact that you were always aware your friend was beside you. Whether you were walking or sleeping or thinking or talking or eating or teasing, you'd know he was with you. Even when your thoughts were a mile away, you would hear him walking—or maybe snoring, if he were asleep. Besides, you would always be conscious of how everything you did would affect your friend. You would be careful of his feelings just because you cared for him. You wouldn't get lost from him, not just for your sake but for his, too. You would know that you were important to him. That would be a warm, good feeling.

This is the way I am going to connect with your question about "praying without ceasing."

To me, the idea behind praying all the time is that you are constantly aware of your Friend who is with you no matter where you are or what you are doing. You talk to Him when you have something to say or ask; you walk along in silence or you do something of your own. But even though you are not actually talking to Him, you are conscious that He is there, interested in whatever you are doing, ready to communicate all the time, keeping you safe, willing to help you at a moment's notice. Even while you are asleep, He is right next to you so if you wake up suddenly He will listen to whatever you have to say. You can do your homework, play, talk to other people all you want and still feel Him right with you like your friend on the backpack trip. Feeling that way makes you free to talk at any instant, even without words, just as you sometimes nudge your friend or raise an eyebrow at him. Nothing is ever too big or too little for you to mention. You don't talk all the time, of course, but the attitude of having a very good Friend close by is what I think of as "praying without ceasing."

*His state was divine, yet he did not cling to his equality
with God but emptied himself to assume the condition of
a slave, and become as we are; and being as all men are, he
was humbler yet, even to accepting death, death on a cross.
But God raised him high and gave him the name which is
above all other names so that all beings in the heavens, on
earth and in the underworld, should bend the knee at the
name of Jesus and that every tongue should acknowledge
Jesus Christ as Lord, to the glory of God the Father.*
—Philippians 2:6-12

Chapter 8

The King

Why do prayers in church sound so different from mine?

"Y'know, some of the things you've been telling me
about prayer don't fit together too hot." Jim's voice was
apologetic. "I mean, I was in church and . . . well, it didn't
all fit." His eyes hoped I'd understand and not be angry. I
was touched that he cared. Some people his age would have
been looking for something about which to disagree, just on
general principles.

"For example?"

"Well, when it was time to pray, everybody bowed their
heads and put their hands in their laps. Or else some of
them knelt down. Then the preacher started his prayer:
'Dear God,' like a letter he was reading. You've been talking about God being my Friend and He . . . well, He *does*
seem like a Friend to me. Only doesn't anybody in church
ever think of Him as their Friend? Like on that backpacking trip we talked about? I mean, it's like there are two
Gods, or something."

I kept from laughing at Jim's conglomerate of self-
expression because underneath I knew exactly what was
bothering him. I have been bothered myself at times by formal rituals and long, showy prayer that seemed to be telling
God what He must do and how to run His world. Somewhere inside I had resolved it to my satisfaction. But telling
it to Jim was something I wasn't sure I could do. Yet, if
prayer were to be real to Jim, he would have to reconcile the
kind of prayer relationship we had been discussing and the
thing he was experiencing in church. Lord, if anybody
straightens this out for Him, it will have to be *you*.

FOR JIM:

Long ago most of the countries of the world had kings.
Besides that they had, usually, slaves who took care of the
work and were mostly treated more like horses or cattle
than like people. The kings, on the other hand, were very
well treated—to the best of everything. Often, too, they
made all the rules to suit their fancy. Of course there were
other people who were neither slaves nor king: tradesmen
and people who worked with their hands, students, religious leaders, entertainers, stablemasters and such. Even
these all had to do exactly what the king required of them.
It was customary for the king to make his subjects bow
down to him and do other actions to show that they knew he
was king and thought he was special. They even acted certain ways to prove that they were his friends and not planning to hurt him, like folding their hands. (Folded hands
can't shoot an arrow, you see.) Some kings required kneel-
ing. Some even demanded that everyone in the kingdom
fall on his face and not raise his eyes when the king came
by.

All of these things were for the purpose of showing the king and everyone else besides that he was considered the best and the greatest and the most revered person in the kingdom. We have inherited and kept on using some of the same kind of demonstrations to indicate that we honor someone special, just as we sometimes keep a picture we have had in our family for generations and hang it on the wall.

Now let's think for a minute about your backpacking friend. On the trip, you both wore old clothes. You were comfortable with each other. You enjoyed having nobody else around so you could talk about anything you wanted to, tease, laugh, or even cry if that's what you felt like doing. It was a very close, affectionate time.

Now suppose you came back from the trip and school started. Imagine your friend was a Boy Scout who had earned the Eagle Rank. Besides that, he had taken part in saving someone's life and had earned a medal from the mayor. Imagine that the time had come for him to have a ceremony and be made an Eagle Scout and at the same time be presented with the mayor's medal.

Everyone would meet together, dressed in special clothes. There would be a ceremony in which several people spoke or read what they had to say and in which they made it clear that they were giving honor to your friend for his special achievements. There might be music of a significant nature which related to all the other things being done. The mayor would probably give a flowery talk along with the presentation of his medal.

None of these would be very much like the conversations you had had with your friend in your sleeping bags at night or eating your dried beef on a rock along the trail. The words would be more formal. People would be dressed differently and either sitting or standing in specific positions, doing the same things at the same time, if that is what had been written into the ceremony (like "The Pledge of Allegiance" and "The Star Spangled Banner"). That kind of behavior would be fitting and proper to honor your friend for his achievements, like people long ago used to honor their king. Still he would be the very same friend with which you had fun and hikes and songs and tears in the wilderness alone. You would be treating him differently on this occasion because you would be joining your friends in honoring him.

We have done the same thing with God in church. We have borrowed, or maybe inherited, some rituals from the long-distant past which we use when we get together to honor our Friend for His special achievements. We bow and fold our hands or we kneel as people did long ago to do homage to a king, because we are honoring the King of kings: God, Jesus, the Holy Spirit (the Trinity). The words we read or say are the most formal words we know to express our awareness that our Friend has all kinds of accomplishments of which we know and for which we want to pay Him tribute. The fact that we do it on a special occasion doesn't change our day-to-day relationship with our Friend anymore than going to the auditorium to watch your other buddy receive his Eagle Scout award and his lifesaving medal would change your friendship. If anything, it would make your love for him deeper to have been a part of a group which said, "We appreciate what you have done."

Next time you go to church, you might think of what is happening as your chance to give honor and glory to the Friend you enjoy so much alone in the wilderness. Then you can do whatever is required by the ceremony just to show your Friend and everybody else that you really do know He is *King*.

In his body lives the fullness of divinity, and in him you too find your own fulfilment, in the one who is the head of every Sovereignty and Power.—Colossians 2:9

Chapter 9

The Idea

Why do we say God answered prayer when it seems like something we've done ourselves?

"I've got some good news for you! Good news! Good news!" Jim was shouting from the back porch as he struggled out of coat and overshoes. In spite of his excitement, he had stopped to help my husband feed the calves. I cut a piece of warm gingerbread. Thank you, Lord. I knew you'd come through.

"Well, tell me." I handed him the gingerbread and pulled a straw out of his tousled hair.

"Dad has a job an' it's really a good one." He paused and I detected a tiny thread of disappointment in his voice. "Only God didn't find it for him."

"He didn't? Then who did?"

"He did himself. He was watching this kid friend of ours with somethin' wrong with his leg, so he has to have a big brace thing on all the time. So he went home and started drawin' plans and thinking about it. And in the middle of the night, he said, an idea woke him up: he saw how to fix the right kind of a brace for the kid's leg. He didn't have anything else to do, so he built one. Then the doctor liked it so much he sent another kid and then a man. Now the company that builds braces wants Dad to work for them full time."

I had to turn away to hide the tears of joy over this story. God didn't give him a job, Jim thinks? O Jim. What did you expect?

Aloud I asked, "Where do you think your dad got the idea that woke him up in the middle of the night?"

"Out of his own head. He thought of it."

"Then who do you suppose made his head—his brains and his memory and his creative imagination?"

Jim paused for a long moment, munching his gingerbread. Then his face lit up like a sunrise.

"Well, if you put it like that, God did. I guess I was expecting a miracle, wasn't I?"

"You were; and you got one. It is no less a miracle for your dad to think up his own idea than for God to give him some sort of supernatural vision on a cloud or something."

I paused. It seemed to me that I had heard this kind of conversation before—and from people older than Jim.

Two hunters lost in the upper pasture had missed the fact that as they prayed, the Lord was sending a guide in the form of a young neighbor who knew the area.

My friend thought she'd "found it herself" after she asked me to pray for her lost billfold.

Often we forget to thank the One who comes to our rescue unless He comes with a flash of lightning and a clap of thunder. Jim, my boy, you are about to hear a little lecture.

FOR JIM:

One of the beautiful things about God's world is that He gave us all the capacity to enjoy each other. We all have good ideas and happy thoughts, sometimes, to share with our friends. We all need each other, too. In fact, some day when God's perfect Kingdom has come, we'll all care for and help each other all the time. Even right now we can be part of one another's lives in a great way.

Your father found his idea in his own creative imagination. But what do you think started that imagination to work? Wasn't it the need of another person? It was a child who was helpless that stimulated your father to care enough to think up something to do for him. Then he went on and cared enough to do it, even though he never thought about being paid or ending up with a good job as a result. God honored his efforts by blessing his creativity—which God put in him to begin with. In a way, the little crippled kid was the answer to your prayer just as much as your father's idea and the company which hired him. They are all parts of God's big plan: the plan of love.

Have you ever gone to visit a friend and had him say to you, "Wow! I was just wishing you'd come"? That gives a pretty good feeling. You feel as if you are important. You are especially loving to your friend because you know he wanted you and you picked that moment to arrive. There's not a whole lot of difference between having him say, "I wished you'd come" and, "I was praying you'd come." In either case, *you* were the answer to his need. It is much better for you to be the answer to your friend's prayer than for whatever he needed to arrive in a flash of bright light or out of the woodwork like magic.

Being the answer to someone's need is exciting. It's like when you are in a play and the star needs an old sunbonnet. She goes to old crippled Mrs. Jenkins and asks to borrow one from her attic. Mrs. Jenkins comes to the play, even if she can hardly walk, and is interested just because she knows that *her* sunbonnet is there in the action. If I know that I may be the answer to someone's prayer, then I am excited and interested to see what God is doing in that person's life. And if I am excited and interested, the other person knows it and feels good about it. We begin to care about each other. Another way of saying, "We care about each other" is to say, "We love each other." Looking for the answers to prayers right in the middle of what we are doing and the people we are with is more exciting, in a way, than waiting for a "miracle" to happen from clear outside.

I never know when I am going to *be* a miracle instead of just seeing one. And when I have a need, I have a lot of fun watching to see who or what is going to arrive on the scene to be my answered prayer. It's more surprising, sometimes, than any mystery you can think of.

I'm not saying that God doesn't sometimes give us miracles that are entirely unexpected and out-of-the-blue, so to speak. Those are exciting, too. But if we get so busy looking for them that we forget the other kind, then we miss a lot of the joy of being alive in God's world. We miss the happy feelings that come when we see a miracle unfolding right in the middle of our friends.

Our Father which art in heaven, Hallowed be thy name.—Matthew 6:9 (KJV)

Chapter 10

Old English

What does the Lord's Prayer mean?

Jim and his sisters came home from church with us to eat before going skiing. In the hurry of fixing the meal, helping seven children round up mittens, ski boots, wax, sweaters and such, I didn't pay a lot of attention to Jim. His sisters were bubbly, talkative girls, laughing with our three girls; Walter was busy getting ready, and Jim was usually quiet. This day, I finally realized, he was more than commonly withdrawn into his own thoughts. He had been sitting near me during church and had listened with great care. I wondered what his next question would be, for I had long since realized that he was actively working on questions to ask me. Does he hope I won't be able to answer? I wondered. Is he playing a game? Maybe. But in the interest of deepening both of our lives, I was willing to go along with him.

"Can I sit by you on the way to the ski hill?"

Jim had a way of dipping from manhood to child so fast I could hardly tell where he was. Was he a little boy today, afraid of losing his mother and wanting me to be near as the best available substitute? Shelving my questions in favor of getting going, I pushed into the car and Jim jumped in beside me.

"It's the Lord's Prayer," he said before we were well

under way. "I don't like it. It sounds like a magic formula that we all have to repeat or we won't get our wish. What's it really mean? Anything?"

His words shot me back to the days when I was Jim's age sitting in church with my parents. I remember trying to put the Lord's Prayer into my own kind of English so it would make more sense to me—and giving up because the intonation always made me sleepy. I laughed. Abracadabra. I knew what Jim meant. Still, the Lord's Prayer is special. There is power and meaning and even a great deal of deep emotion when a group of people prays it together.

"I feel as if I'm bad when I don't say it. But when I say it, I just want to laugh. 'Our Father WHICH . . .' You don't call anybody 'which.' "

Lord, help me show Jim some of the depth of what you were telling us when you gave us this prayer.

FOR JIM:

First, let's remember that even though many of the churches and even more of the people in their own private lives are using new translations of the Bible, most of us still pray the Lord's Prayer in Old English. We do because so many people have learned it thus. The words just flow along the way we have been saying them since we were old enough to talk; and changing them would be very hard. However, using Old English for just that one prayer makes it even more difficult to understand. So many of us just don't try.

We say, *"Our Father which [or who] art in heaven"* to make it known that at that moment we are not talking to our earthly father, but to Someone above all else who created us in the first place. In a way we are also saying that we know we are somebody special because we have Him for a

Father. And having such a Father puts us in a big family along with all the other people who have Him for their Father. So we are, whether we like it or not, all brothers and sisters.

"Hallowed be thy name" is like the Boy Scout ceremony: it is a way of expressing that we admire and respect our Father God more than we know how to tell. Even His name is special. In fact, there is a lot of power in just saying the name of God; it is a way of asking Him to make himself known to us in a personal way, the same as Jesus did for you.

"Thy kingdom come" is a phrase which reminds us (I don't think we need to remind God) that He has a bigger-than-we-understand plan for us and the whole world and we want to help Him keep it going. At least we surely don't want to stand in its way. Just saying we know there is a good plan for everything that happens helps us not to worry when our lives don't seem to be going to suit us.

"Thy will be done on earth, as it is in heaven" also reminds us that God is truly in control. He is managing the universe and He is taking care of us, too. When we pray that part of the prayer, it is good for us to think big—to concentrate on how well God has planned everything from galaxies to the atoms in a grain of sand. His big plan is just too much for our understanding, and in saying so in the prayer, we free ourselves from worrying about it.

But God isn't just interested in the big things. He cares for our needs too. So Jesus told us to be honest about what we have to have. *"Give us this day our daily bread. . . ."* A long time ago in the wilderness, God gave the people manna to eat. He told them not to be pigs about it but to take just enough for each day and He would send what they needed the next (except they were to gather double the day before the Sabbath so they wouldn't have to work on the Sabbath day). If they tried to get extra for saving, it would spoil. We talk about daily bread in the prayer to remind ourselves that God will take care of each day as it arrives. I think when Jesus said "bread" He wasn't just saying "food" but was also telling us to do the best we know how each day and *not worry* about any of our needs tomorrow. Jesus called himself "the bread of life," so when we have Him with us and in us, we have a special kind of food. It is a mystery hard to understand, yet we know that when we have taken Jesus into our lives, we seem to grow all over, in our minds and in our spirits as well as in our bodies.

"Forgive us our debts [or trespasses]" is easy because we all know we do a lot of things we don't really want to do and need to be forgiven for. But the next phrase stops a lot of people: *"as we forgive those who trespass against us."* It sounds as if God is an old meanie who won't forgive us unless we're able to forgive others. Sometimes we can't or don't even want to.

But forgiveness is funny. It is like a jar full of something. You can't put something else into the jar until you have emptied out what was there first. If a person's jar is full of unforgiveness and resentment, there just isn't any room for God's forgiveness to be in it. He is willing. Each one of us has to make room to accept forgiveness. And how do we do it? That is what is important. We have to ask Jesus to go in and help us empty out all the ugliness and be able to forgive and love. It isn't easy to ask for help to forgive when we often don't feel like it. But that's the only way to make room to accept God's forgiving love inside.

"Lead us not into temptation" is another hard phrase. It sounds as if we thought God would deliberately lead us into bad places unless we used a magic formula to ask Him not

to. The new translators of this phrase tell us that what we are really doing is asking God not to let us be tested too hard because we know we aren't very strong by ourselves. Admitting our faults is a very important part of praying. If we admit that we need Him to help, then we allow ourselves to be helped. You know how hard it is to help someone who keeps saying, "I can do it. I can do it."

"*And deliver us from evil*" is one good way of acknowledging that we know the world is full of evil. We need to remind ourselves every day of the truth that we need protection against it. Jesus told us that if we deliberately ask God to protect us from evil we will be safe from having it sneak up on us unawares.

All churches don't end the Lord's Prayer the same way. Ours says, "*For thine is the kingdom and the power and the glory forever.*" We'll talk just about that. I think the last phrase is a reminder to ourselves that we have prayed to a God who cares, have taken note of the things we consider most important: daily needs, forgiveness, and safety, and can now turn it all over to Him who is bigger and wiser than we and who knows everything forever. The last phrase is like a sigh of thankfulness and love. Our Father is loving and tender, but He is the King forever. We can safely turn our lives over to Him and let ourselves appreciate His glory. Glory is bigness and beauty as well as tenderness. It is light, knowledge, perfection.

"*Amen.*" And what does "amen" mean? It means, "I agree. So be it. That's what I want, too."

What god can compare with you: taking fault away, pardoning crime, not cherishing anger forever but delighting in showing mercy? Once more have pity on us, tread down our faults; to the bottom of the sea throw all our sins.
—Micah 7:18, 19

Chapter 11

The Blackboard

What is forgiveness?

"Jim, you're being such a pain that nobody can stand you. Why don't you stop pestering the girls and come into my study for a while?" I scooped up the cookie jar and some napkins and led the way to a secluded spot. "What's bothering you, anyhow?"

Jim followed meekly. I had the feeling that, old as he was, he would have liked a good excuse to cry. Tormenting little sisters seems to be a universal symptom for bigger boys with troubles. And I knew I'd better diagnose the ailment before much longer for our combined sanity. We sat down with cookies and the door shut. For a long time there was silence. Finally Jim spoke.

"What's forgiving, really?"

"I can't answer that unless I know what you are truly asking, Jim. Why do you need to know?"

A strange look crossed his face. I think it was relief. He had some awful secret worry and as the authority figure, I had come to his rescue and ordered him to divulge it. He was no longer responsible.

"Well, I overheard my mom talking to my dad. She said, 'I think I'd get well if your folks would just forgive me.'

She's been sick a long time, so if that's what they need to do, I wish they'd do it. Only what—what *is* it?"

What is forgiving? Lord, what *is* forgiving? How can I answer this earnest young man when I'm not entirely sure myself? I need some help and I need it quickly.

We sat in silence for a while, munching our cookies. Into my mind came the vision of a large blackboard covered with fine writing. A hand moved across it, erasing just as teachers do at the end of the day. The answer to my question? I opened my mouth and began to tell Jim what I was only just seeing for myself.

FOR JIM:

When one person does something to another that hurts, it is as if he makes a sore spot inside. At first the sore spot might get a bit infected and ooze and throb for a time. Then, later, it heals over and leaves a scar. All the time it is healing it is tender, just as a finger that has been infected is easily hurt. The sore spot in one's insides has to be handled carefully. One has to be choosy about what he thinks of, says, and does in order not to make it send a jab of pain into it. Gradually this gets better, but always there will be some more or less tender scar tissue involved. You know there are certain things that have happened to you that you have to be careful thinking about even after several years, sometimes. Well, if someone hurt you very badly, it is like that; you just have to be careful with your feelings.

Now if you think about the person who hurt you over and over again and go over how he hurt you, that makes the pain worse. It hardly has a chance to heal, let alone form scar tissue. When one does that, he is being unforgiving in the very worst sense. He is doing an ugly thing like continually pulling the scab off a healing sore and making it bleed. Sores in our feelings truly are very much like sores on our bodies.

Constantly remembering something that another person has done to one keeps the sore open. If we stop pulling at it, any sore will usually heal after a time. To many people, "forgiving" is nothing more than making themselves quit teasing the sore spot that was caused when somebody hurt them.

God's kind of forgiving, though, is different altogether; and He wants us to accept the help of the Holy Spirit in order to forgive the way He does. If there were a whole blackboard full of writing which a big eraser came and wiped off completely, the blackboard would be blank. There would be no way to find out what had been there. That is what God does when He forgives. Not only that, any harm which has been done He turns into some kind of good. We can't possibly do God's kind of redeeming and forgiving on our own. What we have to do is ask Him to do it for us. He will. He will send forgiveness through us and clear away the ugliness inside, even fill it with love if we'll let Him.

It's funny but it seems to be true that unforgiveness is like a rock. Where it is, nothing else can be. We can't have love and joy and peace and happiness in the spot where the unforgiveness is inside of us. And somehow the hard rock inside one person keeps love from flowing from him to others, too. I think that is what your mother meant when she said she would get well if her in-laws would forgive her. She needed them to let God erase the whole situation, whatever it was, and melt the blocks that were stopping the love of the Lord from flowing freely among the members of the family.

Another funny thing that happens when someone can't

forgive is that one unforgiving thought makes another, like the division of cells you have looked at under the microscope. If somebody can't forgive me, then I have a hard time forgiving him for not forgiving me. And my best friend sees that we have not forgiven each other, so she also has a hard time forgiving us for having unkindnesses in our hearts. Sometimes, a huge ball of unforgiveness gets started in a community or a family and makes everybody feel ugly. Nobody can do anything about it without the Holy Spirit to help. However, Jesus called Him "the Helper" and if we ask Him, He will certainly come to our assistance.

Forgiving links us with God because it is one of the aspects of love, which He is. When we call for help to forgive and the Helper comes, we have all sorts of new awareness of how good and loving God is. We feel closer to His Son and to other people. Forgiving is a lot like taking a bath and washing your hair and putting on all clean clothes. You feel like a party when it is done. A stone is gone from inside and all the dirt is washed from the outside.

There is one other part of forgiving that is important. We know God has made us and given us our circumstances. Sometimes when we don't like ourselves or where we are or whom we live with, we tend to be mad at God and blame Him. We can get a full-grown rock of unforgiveness going toward God himself. It is hard to admit that I haven't forgiven God for making me the way I am or for putting me in the family He did, if I feel that way toward Him. Still, if I don't admit it and ask Him to help me forgive Him, too, I will likely go around with a square black hardness in my insides which hurts and keeps love out. People talk a lot about asking God to forgive them for their bad deeds. Sometimes I think they—and all of us—forget that we have to deliberately forgive Him, too, and if we don't, we can't accept His love for us.

You are wondering, I'm sure, what you can do about the feeling your mother had about her in-laws. You love her and you want them to let go of anything keeping her from getting well. You are even tempted to feel unforgiving toward them for helping prolong her sickness. God knows all of those thoughts. You aren't going to hide any of them from Him. But one good thing about prayer for forgiveness is that as soon as one spot of the ugliness is healed and is filled with God's pure love, it is easier for the spots next to it to begin to heal, too. You can't go inside of your mother or your relatives; but you can open all of your own insides to God and ask Him to cure any unforgiveness that might be there. Maybe He will show you somebody you are holding a grudge against or have been mad at without forgetting. If He does, and you ask Him to help you forgive and entirely erase that hurt, it will help the other members of your family, too. When Jesus was dying on the cross, He asked God to forgive those who were killing Him so unmercifully. His actions let us see how very important forgiveness is in our lives.

No one has ever seen God; but as long as we love one another God will live in us and his love will be complete in us.—*1 John 4:12*

Chapter 12

Love Energy

Does God hear lots of people better than a few?

The door opened a crack, letting in a blast of wintry wind and a very red-nosed boy. My son had come in earlier and I had wondered what was keeping Jim out on the coldest evening of the year. As he stood rubbing his icy hands, I felt a tension about him. Something deep was happening in his life, something holy and scary and beautiful. I waited while he blew on his fingers and rubbed his ears. Finally he sat down on the stool and leaned his elbows on the counter where I was rolling out a pie crust.

"Twenty-five people are coming to my mom's tonight to pray for her to get well. They're all coming at once and that's what I want to ask you about. Do I go or stay here, and what's going to happen? Why is it better for so many people to come? Does God answer prayers better the more numbers of people pray?" His eyes were bright with excitement and perhaps fear. I could sense his desire to hope and his dread of perhaps being disappointed if he dared expect anything. I understood.

What if, I caught myself thinking, what if she doesn't improve? What if God's answer is *no*? O Lord, I believe. Help my unbelief. Help me trust *you* that you know what sort of healing she needs and that you give it to her.

"Do you want to hear what I think about it?"

"I'm scared to."

I looked at Jim in surprise. "Why?" He sat quietly playing with a bit of dough on the counter.

"If you believe she'll get well and she doesn't . . ." His eyes spoke the question I myself had been asking.

"Then what will happen to your own relationship with God?" I finished for him. He nodded. I took a deep breath. All the things we'd said about prayer were now on the line for Jim. Was it magic or was it power, a game or reality? Lord, *help!*

FOR JIM:

No matter who we are, how "bad" or "good," rich, poor, smart, dumb, every person has a bit of love inside him. Maybe he only loves his dog or his goldfish. But nobody is completely without a thread of love. The Bible tells us that God *is* love. Jesus is God, so He is love, too. The Holy Spirit is part of the Trinity, so He, too, is love. God created each person in His image; so He must have put a spot of love in each of us. I am not talking now about the kind of love we call "romantic." I am talking about the kind that cares for and wants everything good for each person, no matter what—the way Jesus did when He died on the cross to free us from the burden of our sins.

When a person prays, he connects the streak of love within himself to the Creator of love, the person of Love: God. Just as the power of the wires in the wall is connected to the lamp when we plug in the cord, prayer connects the loving nature inside each of us with the pure, strong love of God. If I concentrate the full strength of my human love on you and then plug into God's love, I am beaming a power in your direction like a giant spotlight. Suppose I put my hands on you and focus not only my own love on you but ask God to let my hands be a channel for His love to touch you, too. There is a great deal of energy in love coming through to you.

Now suppose there are twenty-five people with their human love plugged into God's power and all concentrating on the same person at the same time. Can you imagine what a lot of energy is flowing into that person?

We don't know exactly what your mother's body, emotions, mind, or spirit needs, but I can just see the love coming in to fill the needs and make her better. We don't know the timetable for her healing, either. We can, though, be sure without a doubt that *something* will happen in her body from that jolt of love that the twenty-five people will ask there when they pray for God's healing power.

As for your being there: do you want to be part of a channel for God's love and add your hands and your prayers? if so, go ahead. If you are shy, God will understand, since He knows you perfectly. (Of course He does. He made you!)

We can't put a limit on what God is going to do in your mother's life by expecting any certain result from the prayers tonight. I won't go over tomorrow and tell her to do the family laundry because I know she's completely well. On the other hand, I am positive she will be different after her experience. And I wouldn't be surprised if I did go over and found her washing clothes. You can never be sure how God is going to answer prayers. All you can be sure of is that He *does* answer them. It is up to you to watch carefully so you won't miss what He is doing not only in your mother's life but also in the lives of the twenty-five people who come to pray. We belong to such a big family we sometimes forget to watch everyone for the good things God accomplishes.

*When the day comes—it is Yahweh who speaks—the
heavens will have their answer from me, the earth its answer
from them, the grain, the wine, the oil, their answer from
the earth, and Jezreel his answer from them. I will sow him
in the country, I will love Unloved; I will say to No-People-
of-Mine, "You are my people," and he will answer, "You
are my God."—Hosea 2:21-24*

Chapter 13

The Volcano

Can an unbeliever stop prayer from working?

The phone rang at seven-fifteen in the morning. I answered amid egg frying and sack-lunch preparations. At
first I wasn't sure it was Jim's voice I was hearing.

"Even though I was over yesterday and Mom says I
shouldn't come so often or you'll get tired of me, can I still
come on the bus after school today and talk to you about
something?" He said it all in one breath and I heard his intense concern in the small gasp that followed. I had been
glad for his decision to go home the evening before, even
though I wasn't at all sure he'd have the courage to be with
the group praying for his mother. His relationship with
Jesus and his dependence on the Holy Spirit were new and
tender. I thought he might not have wanted to expose them
to the grown-ups who had been involved.

I had joined the prayers for Jim's mother from my home,
aware that my loving participation would further imple-
ment the healing. In fact, I had called my prayer partner to
ask for her support. I believe, from many impressive experiences, that power flows through the prayers of believers, no

matter where they are. It soaks and touches with the love
we are a part of and are asking for.

"Of course, Jim. Catch the bus and we'll take you home
before bedtime. And don't forget your homework."

He laughed. I guess I sounded like a mother. Maybe
mothers do tend to behave like mothers, no matter whose
children are involved. Jim had been at our house so much I
automatically treated him as one of my own.

All day I thought about Jim and his family: his new delicate love of the Lord and the plans I was sure God must
have for him. When he finally arrived with my children on
the bus, I could hardly wait to see what had happened.

Everybody had to have a snack and give me a rundown
on the day's activities. We had to fix a hole in a book bag
and hunt for a notebook. There were calves to feed and hay
to put out for an ailing horse. Finally Jim was back with a
moment of quiet. He stood, tense with worry.

"What is it, Jim?"

"Well, it was really neat at first, last night. In fact the
part with Mom was all good. Afterwards she said it was hot
where people's hands were touching her and she felt so
much power she knew something had happened. All the
people crowded around and some prayed out loud and some
just stood quietly. I really liked it. Mom said it felt like a
yellow blanket of love covering her all over. But then afterward . . ." He hesitated. I could feel his fear and his face
was a puzzle. Finally he took a deep breath and continued.

"Well, my big sis had a friend visiting. Nobody in the
family likes her, really, but Sis says this girl—Angie's her
name—hasn't any friends and Sis always brings that kind
of people home, you know."

I nodded. I am a bringer in of stray kittens myself, and
Jim's sister's action had already touched my heart. Some-

times the stray kitten scratches, though. I know from experience.

"Anyhow, after Mom was in bed we were talking—well, Angie and Sis were, and I was listening, and she said, 'That's all silly. And it won't work, either. You know why?' We were both kind of mad at her. I could tell Sis was, and I know I was. But what Angie said next was so crazy. I've got to know if it's true."

"What did she say?"

"She said that prayer wouldn't work because she didn't believe in it and whenever there was someone in the house that didn't believe it, that jinxed it and nothing could happen. That's not true, is it?"

I gave Jim a quick hug and pulled out a stool for him to relax while I stirred up a cake. Poor Jim. This seemed like a low blow for him. Still, inside, I was happy because the old ugly prayer-is-magic notion had come out in the open again so we could deal with it once more. The ages have all had their problems separating magic from power, real from make-believe. Lord, please help me steer Jim into a greater knowledge of what love really is—the power of the universe.

FOR JIM:

Let's suppose some little boys are playing with matches and start a fire with a handful of grass. Their mother, who is watching from the house, sees it and runs with a bucket of water to put out the fire. Maybe she spanks the boys. Maybe she only explains to them how dangerous it is to play with fire. Perhaps she makes them light another fire, with her there to watch, and find out for themselves how hot and painful it can be. Probably for a long time the boys remember their lesson and leave fire alone.

The little boys grow older, and later there comes a time when they need to use fire. They make all the proper arrangements ahead of time, carrying plenty of water to have ready to pour on the fire and put it out when they are done using it. They know that if they have plenty of water and keep their fire in its proper place, they can keep control of it. For a long time they think they don't have to be afraid of fire if they keep enough water around.

Maybe one later day the boys see a big building burning out of control. They watch the firemen try to put it out and not succeed—maybe not for a whole day. Finally, when most of the building is gone, the tired firemen can apply enough water to finish it off. The boys get a different picture of fire at that point. They realize how powerful it is and that sometimes nobody can put it out, even with great quantities of water.

Now, suppose one more thing. Suppose there is a volcano erupting molten lava and fire and ashes all down the mountainside. Most likely the firemen who worked tremendously hard, pouring water on the building fire for hours, won't even take their hoses up to try to put out the volcano. The volcano is caused by the heat at the core of the earth, making its way through a weak spot in the side of the mountain and breaking through to the outside. It is connected to the very center of the earth, and no amount of water would make any difference to it. The water might boil and make clouds of steam if somebody put some of it on the volcano. But the volcano would be hot as long as it was going to.

Do you think I got a bit off the subject of Angie and prayers for your mother? Well, I didn't. God's love is the very core of things, like the heat in the volcano. It is the center of the world—yes, and the whole universe. Like the volcanic heat, there is nothing in the world that can put it out because it *is* the heart of everything. People have always had trouble understanding the size of God's love. God sent Jesus to show us what love is like. He showed us by dying for our sins and then coming back to let us see that sin isn't able to exist where love is. He showed us that when we make mistakes or do damage, love can change it into good. His life let us see how love is more powerful than anything else. The more we read the Bible, the better we understand that God is love and love is the power that always wins over anything which is less than love.

Angie must have gotten into the group of people who think of prayer as magic. They think we are making things happen by incantations (formulas that we say) and that we have to do everything exactly right for the magic to work. That is not the way it is at all. When people pray to God, they are joining their love to His and getting in touch with the power at the center of the universe. When we get in touch with that power, we are connected to something so big and powerful that anybody's little doubts or bad feelings would be just exactly as effective as one drop of water would be against a volcano.

People who pray in love to the God of love are hooked up to something so much bigger than they are that it's silly to think they can control it. We don't control God with our prayers. You know that already. And we don't control Him with our doubts either. He knows exactly what is best for your mother. All of us who are praying for her are concentrating love on her by hooking ourselves up to the original power supply. Nothing can ever change that love, nor stop it, either.

What we need to do is let God's love show through us all to Angie so she will see how great it is and want it for herself. She can quit doubting then, and join in with the rest of us to experience the power of God's love. We can pray for her quietly so she doesn't even know it, plug into the love network, and beam it on her until she thinks differently. It's better to be on fire with God's love than all wet, don't you think? I do.

*The blessing cup that we bless is the communion with
the blood of Christ, and the bread that we break is a
communion with the body of Christ. The fact that there is only
one loaf means that, though there are many of us, we form
a single body because we all have a share in this one loaf.*
—*1 Corinthians 10:16, 17*

Chapter 14

The Flashlight

How does the prayer book fit in with real praying?

"It's for you, Mom. It's Jim."

I was busy and tired when he called and I realized I
didn't really want to have a prayer question from Jim that
particular Saturday morning. Although I was well aware
that my answers to his questions were coming regularly
from more than me, the exhilaration and subsequent drain
from each encounter let me see that I needed to take some
time to recharge my own batteries in preparation. I was re-
lieved when, instead, he asked if he could play with my son.
"Why doesn't he find some friends more his own age?" I
wondered crossly. My children were all younger. "Why
doesn't he?" Suddenly, out of the depths of me came a
warm glow of love for Jim.

"Of course," I said aloud, strangely over both my fa-
tigue and my irritation. We loved him and he knew it. Love
has no age requirements.

"Of course you can come. You are always welcome,
Jim."

The boys became immediately involved in a game in
Walter's room. I didn't think Jim had shared his prayer

quest with his younger friend. It seemed to involve mostly him and me—and the Lord. Still, kids often communicate in ways I don't understand. The boys were playing with flashlights on the ceiling, the curtains drawn. They were deep in their own talk, punctuated by laughter. I let them slip totally out of my consciousness.

"Mom, come here, can you?" Walter's voice was serious. I went at once. His room was a sacred place for our heart-to-heart discussions, and it would have been useless to ask him to come to me. The boys were lying on the upper bunk and apparently Jim had told of his search for "truth" about prayer.

"One thing that doesn't seem to fit is the prayer book." It seemed the discussion had hit a snag and both boys were determined to straighten it out.

"The prayer book?"

"In church we read stuff out of the prayer book and sometimes everybody is reading the same thing at once. It doesn't seem like some of it even matters or makes sense. All the ways we've been thinking about God get sort of mixed up in the prayer book and I don't understand it."

The question stopped me, too. I could remember days when I disliked reading prayers or even responsive readings. Sing-song, uninflected voices droning through written prayers left me cold. Yet they were there. They were real. Nobody had removed them from the service. Lord, you will have to help me say whatever the boys will understand and need to hear about this. And do you mind if I listen, too?

FOR JIM:

We've talked before about how prayer is a way of helping beam the force of love in a certain direction like a spotlight. God wills for us to participate in this love, and when we pray, we are joining with Him not only in participating in it ourselves, but in spotlighting someone else's needs. There are many needs in every life in every part of the world. Nobody knows all of the things God would like for us to pray for (and thank Him for, as well). People have had hints and, with the help of the Holy Spirit, have written their ideas down. These ideas have been collected into prayer books which many churches use.

Think of a group of people each holding a small pencil flashlight as you were just doing. Nobody could make much of a light by himself. But suppose everyone decided to focus his flashlight on the same thing. That would make a whole lot of light in one spot. By reading the same prayer from the prayer book that a great many other people are reading, we are focusing our prayers like the many little flashlights.

Besides, no matter how carefully we pray, we could never remember all the matters we need to pray about. We might forget to focus our little flashlights on something very important in our own lives or the lives of other people. The prayers in the book or the back of the hymnal help us not to miss matters of importance.

Let's look for a minute at some of the things in the written prayers. No matter which books we use—the little supplements in the backs of the hymnals or the big prayer books—there are certain classifications. There are prayers for ourselves. Some are confessions of our weaknesses and the things we have done wrong that we might forget. Some are reminding us and telling God again that we want to follow Him and love Him. Some of the prayers are praise and thanksgiving. All of those are personal. Then there are prayers for other Christians all over the world (the Church), for peace, for health, for freedom, for food and other needs.

There are prayers for people who are dying and people who are ill. We would probably forget many of those matters if the prayer books didn't help us.

There's another good reason for using prayer books, too. The church has been around a long time, so there is a lot of church history in it. For some people history is a bore. But if we think of ourselves as one big Christian family, as Jesus told us we are, then the history of our past links us together. As we read from prayer books, we feel as if we are at a big family reunion. Jesus was alive in the lives of the people long ago, and He is alive in our lives right now. We have Him to fasten us together and make us interested in the past experiences of those other Christians.

We've talked before, too, about the fact that some of the funny old language from England's past is still around. In a way that, too, links us to all the people out of the long-ago who loved Jesus and worshipped God just as we are doing ourselves. When we read, we can imagine those people reading with us.

We can look at the prayer book and find an outline for the year. There are happenings in the church calendar all the time. Sometimes we think a lot about them, like during Advent. Sometimes we pass over them lightly, hardly thinking about them at all. Still, they make a pattern which people have followed for many years. Let's look at the calendar a bit.

Have you ever been in a household where a new baby is expected? There are lots of preparations to be made. There are clothes to buy and wash for the baby. A bed must be found and fixed. All kinds of special equipment must be gotten together to make the baby comfortable and happy. Some of it isn't absolutely necessary. Still, it makes taking care of the baby more fun and easier. Advent is getting ready for a new arrival of Christ in our lives. Even though we know He is here all the time, it is fun to see if we can be prepared for the kind of newness and freshness that comes when we are expecting it. It is exciting to see if we can find out some new dimension of Jesus during Advent. The prayers in the section called "Advent" in the book help us see some of the ways that other people have known Jesus.

We celebrate "Epiphany," which is said to be the time when Jesus was made known to the Gentiles. You know originally He came to the Jews, who were looking for their "Messiah." We are not Jews. The date when Jesus offered himself to us, too, is very important to us. Suppose only the Jews could love Him. We would be the saddest people on earth. Epiphany is also the day Jesus was baptized, which is important to everybody.

Lent comes before Easter. The prayer books are full of the joy of getting ready for the biggest event in the Christian church—the resurrection of Jesus from death. We have a lot to think about to be really ready to accept the sacrifice He made to die on the cross for us because He loved us.

Then come the solemn days of Maundy Thursday, when we remember the disciples and Jesus eating together at the Last Supper, and Good Friday when Jesus died on the cross. Dying would be the end of the book if it hadn't been for Easter, when He rose from the dead. Easter is the happiest celebration of the church. It takes all kinds of prayers to help us show our joy at the resurrection of Jesus.

We have a day to celebrate Jesus' ascension back to heaven and a day of Pentecost to remember when the Holy Spirit came to stay for good. Anybody who has had an experience of the love and the power of Jesus through the Holy Spirit loves to remember and celebrate Pentecost.

There are so many ways to love God, to praise Him, to

celebrate His presence, that we could never do them all. We have the help of a whole group of other Christians who wanted to love and praise and celebrate as much as we do. When we read prayers from the book, it is interesting to imagine the long line of people, now gone to be with Jesus in person, reading the lines from our books with us.

*Now Jesus was in one of the towns when a man
appeared, covered with leprosy. Seeing Jesus he fell on his
face and implored him. "Sir," he said, "if you want to, you
can cure me." Jesus stretched out his hand, touched him
and said, "Of course I want to! Be cured!" And the
leprosy left him at once.—Luke 5:12*

Chapter 15

The Gold Light

Does God really heal people today?

The late winter day was cold and still. The phone rang
right after I had finished the morning dishes. I love winter
days—when I can stay at home. But lately I had been unusually busy away from home. I wanted a day all to myself;
so I groaned when I heard the bell. Must I? Of course I
must. People who live on ranches are particularly careful
about answering their telephones. Many times neighbors in
trouble have called and I have thanked God I was there to
help.

The caller was Jim's mother. In spite of the fact that I
was unusually close to Jim, I didn't know his parents very
well. I guess I sensed that he wanted an adult friend who
would not be influenced by the other grown-ups in his life.
Maybe I responded to his need to be treated as an adult
himself. At any rate, I was surprised when she phoned me.

"Jim's sick with a bad sore throat," she said. "He had
planned to go tonight to the high school football game and
go out for pizza afterward, so he is very much upset because
of the illness." She hesitated. I could hear the apology in
her voice. "He says he wants you to come over and pray for

him. I hate to ask you—but I know from experience that it helps. Could you?"

We live out of town. Eight miles of winter-time travel on a cold morning wasn't exactly exciting. However, Jim's spiritual journey *was* exciting. I knew it was important to go.

"Of course. I'll be right there."

On the way, I prayed a bit myself. I have never learned to be entirely comfortable with prayers for physical healing. I *know* it happens; I guess I often see other kinds of health that look so much more important and necessary than physical health that I tend to ignore physical healing. Maybe I just don't have "the gift." On the other hand, I have been part of some tremendous demonstrations of physical cures. I can't deny them; and I don't want to. Somewhere inside me there was a mix-up. I prayed that God would overcome it and do whatever He wanted to, myself and my old hang-ups notwithstanding.

Jim's mother was pretty, though frail. She had a new glow about her that reminded me of her recent experiences with prayer. Jim was feverish and flushed. I sat down beside him. His mother went out and shut the door.

"I have a sore throat and a headache. And I want really much to go to the game tonight. I suppose I don't want any magic—only I guess I really *do* want some." Jim's voice was husky.

I want some too, I thought. Sick children and animals always tear me up. I am grateful that my own children were mostly healthy. I sat quietly for a long time trying to decide how to pray. Suddenly the Holy Spirit reminded me of something. The reminder clicked into place neatly. Thank you, Lord.

FOR JIM:

Prayer is tuning into God's perfect love, you know. When we pray we try to open the channels inside ourselves as well as asking that the areas in other people's lives be filled with new love. Love is not something we can see. We can see the results of it but not the love itself.

God gave us our imaginations, though, so let's use them right now to help His healing love to make you better. First we can imagine Jesus standing with His hands on the sore spots, touching the hurting places just as He did a long time ago when He lived in Palestine. As soon as He touched a sick person, that person was well. The power of Jesus' love cured anything anybody had wrong. There is no difference now. He still has power to heal. We often forget to ask for the power and healing; and often when we remember to ask, we turn it into a negative by feeling sure that we will never get what we have asked for.

As you and I together picture Jesus' hands on the sore places, we can also picture love flowing from His hands into our bodies. Let's do it with your sore throat. Think of Jesus touching your throat on the outside and, as He does, let's visualize the love seeping through the tissues of your neck and moving into every cell inside. Imagine the love as gold light, if you want to. We'll get the doctor book so we can picture it going easily from one organ to the next as His hands touch you. I will help you open up the gold light of love by imagining it with you. What we're doing, Jim, is much more than pretending. Pretending is based on fantasy; our imaginings right now are based on God's truth found in the Bible.

As the love moves from one part of your throat and ears and nose to another, visualize the tender, red tissue becoming normal with all the swelling going down and the fiery redness subsiding. Imagine yourself thanking Jesus in your usual pleasant voice along with putting your poor used handkerchief away because your nose is not running anymore. Think of your ears so healthy that you can hear every sound—even Jesus moving His feet on the carpet of your bedroom. As you practice the imagining, thank Jesus for what He is doing for you. Tell Him how much you love and appreciate Him. Do it just as you would if you were living on the shores of the Sea of Galilee all those years ago—as if you were one of those whom Jesus touched and made whole again. He is the same Jesus even though it is the twentieth century and we have many new inventions and much more medical knowledge. Actually, Jim, isn't it interesting that even with all that amazing knowledge, Jesus still has to be the only cure for the common cold?

After you have finished picturing your own healing, you might like to think of someone else who has a problem and imagine the same kind of thing for him. Concentrating our thoughts on the love of Jesus and then picturing that love flowing over and through another person, healing and clearing up problems, is a good way to pray. You don't always know what is hurting another person or what Jesus needs to heal; but *He* does. If you visualize Him touching and pouring His love through from head to toe, you can hardly pray more effectively for somebody else. If you have friends who are sad or ill or just mean, loving imaginings based on belief in God's power can improve the situation. You can help by being a channel to beam that love in their direction. Then you can assist in the thank-you part of any gift by thanking Jesus yourself.

When God gave us imaginations, He offered us a lovely place to enjoy Him. Nothing is more pleasant than imagining the good, happy, loving things Jesus did when He lived on earth—and does now as well. If our imaginations are filled with Him, then we become creative and full of great ideas for ourselves and our friends. We also become more healthy with lots of energy, able to do the activities we imagine. Will you practice, now, until your sore throat is well?

I am the vine, you are the branches. Whoever remains in me, with me in him, bears fruit in plenty. —John 15:5

Chapter 16

The Free-Flowing Pipe

How should I pray with my family?

Jim agreed to continue the creative-imagination kind of prayer, so after we prayed I chatted with him a bit before sitting down with his mother for a cup of tea in her warm kitchen. She had experienced a beautiful victory in her own life which she was happy to share with me. Her radiance was thrilling. She told me about her husband's job. She communicated her tender appreciation for the gift of it. She told me of her happiness in watching Jim grow spiritually, too. I was standing up to leave when she asked me her own urgent prayer question.

"Will you teach Jim to pray with his mother?"

I was surprised. She had spoken so quietly I had almost missed it. But I felt the urgency in her voice which told of her longing to have her son join her in prayer.

Almost every mother wants that, I thought. But a mother who is battling a possible fatal illness definitely needs it. I should have thought to help my young friend grow into a caring adult who could share his growing with his mother. I gave her a quick hug.

"I'll do my best."

As I thought the matter over, I was not quite sure how to get on with it. This young man needed other close relationships and awarenesses to separate him from his environ-

Successful Living®

Book Mark

Thank you for buying this book! Please help us serve you better by completing and mailing this card!

___I buy Successful Living books at _____

_____

___I've complimented the store manager for carrying these inspirational, family-type books!

___Please send me your catalog.

___I would appreciate spiritual counseling toward a more real and personal relationship with God.

___I will support your ministry with prayer.

___My church would like to have a rack.

___Send details on how to be a Distributor.

___Please send details on your Successful Living home party plan.

NAME_____

ADDRESS_____

_____ ZIP_____

PHONE (   )_____

". . . if you confess with your mouth, 'JESUS IS LORD,' and believe in your heart that God raised HIM from the dead, you will be saved. For it is with your heart that you believe and are justified, and it is with your mouth that you confess and are saved." Romans 10:9,10 [New International Version]

WHAT IS SUCCESSFUL LIVING?

We're an organization which takes a **positive** action distributing inspirational books through dedicated independent Distributors. Want to participate? Mail this card today!

WHY THIS EMPHASIS?

"If religious books are not widely circulated among the masses in this country, I do not know what is going to become of us as a nation. If truth be not diffused, error will be; if God and His Word are not known and received, the devil and his works will gain the ascendancy; if the evangelical volume does not reach every hamlet, the pages of a corrupt and licentious literature will; if the power of the Gospel is not felt throughout the length and breadth of the land, anarchy and misrule, degradation and misery, corruption and darkness, will reign without mitigation or end."

—Daniel Webster, 1823

CALL OR WRITE TODAY!
Your Successful Living Distributor

DAN & BARBARA DAWSON

PHONE (219) 589-2655
423 COMPROMISE ST.
BERNE, IN 46711

AFFIX
POSTAGE

ment. Had Jim come to that point? I knew I could easily spoil our tender closeness through which much of his growing was happening. Our open access to each other and our common touch by the Holy Spirit was too new and delicate to be tampered with. Yet here was a mother in real need and a young son with true sensitivity. Well, Lord, whatever you want me to do, I'll try to accomplish—but *not* on my own.

I waited a few days until the sore throat was only a memory. The game had been won. A debate had gone well. Jim had been pleased with both results and even more pleased with a pair of twins, a boy and girl, who had suddenly become his friends. I was happy with them. They were unspoiled, sensitive youngsters who were growing spiritually just like Jim; and they were exactly his age. I had a feeling he was on the edge of a great spurt of newness, and it was time to edge into his mother's request.

FOR JIM:

We have to watch ourselves all the time to be sure we don't forget that prayer is love. It is not asking and getting. It is participating and learning love from the Source of that love. We talked before about imagining that we were open channels with love running through us like water through pipes. Sometimes pipes have obstructions in them that stop the water. We can picture the love pushing against the obstructions until they start to crumble and are washed away. We can imagine kinks in the pipe being straightened out by the force of the flow of love. We can imagine smaller pipes taking off from the big main ones and still smaller ones taking off from those so that there would be no space anywhere too small to be penetrated by God's love. And we can always picture the light of that love going even where pipes wouldn't fit.

All this pretending, if you want to call it that, going on inside of us helps us to stay aware of the purpose of our lives, which is to be close to God—to be His friends and enjoy His company, to live love. And do you know what else it does? It makes us more and more aware all the time of other people who need love in their lives. Of course everybody does. Nobody on this earth can get along totally without love. We know that; but sometimes things happening in another person's life make it necessary for him to have some extra-special show of love. When you and I are focusing ourselves on the flow of God's love, then it's like when you pour out a big bucket of water. You can see the low places where you know the water will run even before it gets to them. We can see someone else's need and watch the flow of love go to that need.

The very best place to watch for a need-for-love is in one's own family. That's the hardest place to see it, too. The reason is that we become so used to our family members that we forget to really look at and listen to them. Somebody in your family or mine might be really hurting, but because we are so accustomed to them, we forget to notice. I am always sorry when I see that has happened because of my carelessness. I am glad God forgives me and gives me another chance.

There is a kind of prayer which somebody called "soaking prayer." I like the idea. It is a wonderful way to pray for people—almost the same as praying by imagining, which we talked about last week. The difference is that you actually put your hands on another person and imagine the love of Jesus flowing through your hands and seeping into him. It doesn't need to take long or be obvious. It is a way you can pray for your sisters or your father or mother without making anybody feel uncomfortable. God knows what is going on and so do you.

The reason I mentioned this particular kind of prayer to you is because your mother has recently had a rather concentrated "soaking prayer" experience. All of her friends who prayed for her were soaking her with God's love and healing power to help her recover from her illness. It was like going to the doctor's office to have a treatment with some of his big machines. You know, though, that often after such a treatment the doctor tells you, "Go home now and soak the sore spot with hot Epsom Salts, every day."

All of your mother's twenty-five friends were not able to come back day after day. Yet your mother needs some continued "soaking." You are here and you know about prayer. Perhaps you might be able to lend your hands to Jesus to touch her. Later, you might even lend Him your voice to pray aloud with her. Even if you don't tell her the first time you are praying for her, she will know after a while what is making her feel so much better. Sometimes praying aloud with someone else is uncomfortable at first. That is why I suggested slipping into it by "soaking," which is easier. It is also a lot of secret fun. "What will God do with this new love in Mother's life?" you can ask yourself. Then you can watch to see. No prayer is ever wasted, because prayer changes everybody it touches. You are taking part in healing; you are helping to bring warm, precious change. Jesus is smiling at you as you participate with Him in healing. As you are silently talking to Him, the two of you can laugh at whatever good is going on while you soak.

Christians sometimes talk about "brothers and sisters in Christ." Jesus is like the big Brother who makes us all each other's brothers and sisters. While you are quietly praying soaking prayer for your mother, you can enjoy thinking of her as your "Sister in Christ." Jesus is pleased, I'm sure, when a child matures enough to understand how to minister love to his parents even though they must still tell him what he can and can't do because he is their responsibility. Try it and see what happens.

Yahweh, my heart has no lofty ambitions, my eyes do
not look too high. I am not concerned with great affairs or
marvels beyond my scope. Enough for me to keep my soul
tranquil and quiet like a child in its mother's arms, as
content as a child that has been weaned. Israel, rely on
Yahweh, now and always!—Psalm 131

Chapter 17

Daddy's Lap

What is worship?

"I won another debate. And Mary and Marty are going
with me to church on Easter." Jim's voice over the phone
was jubilant. Everything had seemed so tense for him all
winter that I could have jumped for joy at this turn of
events. People like Jim have hard going, it appears to me.
They have these times because the business of growing is so
intensely important that there is no relaxed sliding along
life's highway. I'm that way, too. I'm still pushing for
growth, change, new and better ways to relate to the Lord
and to other people. Things seem hard for me, too. I know I
make them so. But somehow I don't know how not to. In-
tensity has its own rewards, but it asks its payment, too. I
really understood and empathized with him. Even joy can
be so intense it hurts.

Jim was going on over the phone and, lost in my own
thoughts, I was missing what he was saying.

". . . so I want to know something. What *is* worship?"

"Do you want your answer over the phone or shall we
meet tomorrow after school? I have to go grocery shopping
and pick up the girls at the church."

"Tomorrow's okay. Just so I know before Easter."

Why Easter? I wondered. Jim's life is full of self-imposed deadlines.

I met him after school while the girls practiced with the choir and Walter went to Cub Scouts. Jim came bounding up to meet me, his cheeks pink from the cold wind. What is worship, Lord, for this young man? What is true worship for a youth just on the brink of manhood? You will have to help me, for I suspect there are as many kinds of "true" worship as there are days in the year and people on the face of the earth. Yet it is a need common to us all, like water and air.

FOR JIM:

We've talked about many topics this past winter having to do with prayer. Now let's do something different to talk about worship. Let's pretend we're little kids and imagine something.

See if you can remember how it feels to be little—so little that most of what happens is beyond your understanding. Most of your life revolves around yourself and your parents—what *you* need and want is your focus. But what happens to you is mostly controlled by your parents. They feed you and take care of you. You don't even think about it. They give you fun presents, tuck you into your warm bed at night, sometimes discipline you. Still, you expect that; and really you want it because they define your world for you and keep you safe by disciplining you.

Imagine yourself full of good supper topped with ice cream, bathed and dressed in warm pajamas, sitting on your dad's knee. You snuggle down into his warm lap while he reads your bedtime story. Think how comfortable and safe you feel. You don't even have to understand all your daddy has done for you to make you that way. All you know is that, in your baby fashion, you love your daddy immensely. He is, at the moment, your whole world.

One of the ways we worship God is described by our little "pretend." We are encompassed by His love, protection, gifts, comfort. We don't need to be distracted from our joy by anything at all. We can't possibly know all He has done for us; we can't understand what His ultimate plans are or what the future holds. But we can quietly *enjoy* Him, just as the tiny child enjoys his daddy as he holds him in a safe, warm lap. Even when we have had some kind of "discipline," we are happy to be so cared for.

Easter is the day we celebrate the fact that Jesus conquered death. He died and now He lives again. There is a great deal to be understood, and as we try to think about it, we are overcome with awe at the immensity of it all. We aren't really able to understand intellectually what has happened, especially with relation to ourselves. But sitting quietly in His presence, we can happily experience the living Lord who loves each of us enough to die for us on the cross. To me that is why we sing and have trumpet music and flowers and new clothes, even Easter eggs and parties. We are so full of the happiness of our Lord that we don't know enough things to do to express it!

There are lots of ways to worship God. We can sit in church and sing or pray with other people, joining them in honoring Him. We can cry out of sadness and tell Him what we are sad about. Telling Him is trusting Him, and that is an important kind of worship. We can run and play ball or debate or go on a hayride knowing that He is there with us. And that "knowing" is worship because worship means mostly just our increasing awareness that God is everywhere and always a part of everything that goes on.

We can worship by "praising," which is saying, "Father, I know you really *do* know best." Nobody can love God even a little bit without what I call worship: knowing that it is He who is at the center of our lives. Now go to church with your friends and enjoy the presence of our living Lord. Sing and clap and tell Him how glad you are that He is your Friend. There is no better kind of worship.

Open up, open up, clear the way, remove all obstacles
from the way of my people. For thus speaks the Most High,
whose home is in eternity, whose name is holy: "I live in a
high and holy place, but I am also with the contrite and
humbled spirit, to give the humbled spirit new life, to revive
contrite hearts."—Isaiah 57:14, 15

Chapter 18

Family Names

Why do we end our prayers "in Jesus' name"?

Jim and his new friends had hiked all the way from town
to our ranch. Their pink faces and wind-tangled hair told
me it might be nice if I offered to take them home—after a
brief break for refreshments. We sat in the kitchen warming
hands and enjoying hot chocolate with the rest of my children.

The twins were perfect friends for Jim, I thought to myself. They were jolly and enthusiastic, sharing his spiritual
progress but still a great deal more relaxed than he. Some of
their gaiety seemed to rub off on Jim so our time together
was full of smart cracks and funny remarks. They kept my
children in constant gales of giggling, and I didn't try very
hard to stay on the periphery. We often forget just to laugh
and enjoy life—we who are geared high and tense. God
made us with funny bones and my guess is that, yes, they
are holy, too. Since we're made in His image, God must also
have a sense of humor.

"We were talking on the way out," Jim was suddenly
serious. I quickly focused my thoughts, sure he would have
a hard question for me. His questions were getting more

and more adult and thoughtful. I could see real growth in every area of his life.

"We were talking about how prayers are so often ended with 'in Jesus' name.' I'm not sure what that really means. I mean, I suppose I should know, but I guess I don't, nor do Mary and Marty, either." He inclined his head toward them apologetically. I laughed.

"And I suppose you think I know?" They all nodded vigorously. "Well, I'm not so sure. But I'll try. The Holy Spirit will have to help me, though, as He has always done."

FOR JIM:

Names have always been special. In Jesus' day they were even more special than they are now. To know a man's name was to have a certain power over him, and to share names was a bond of unity between two people. Jesus' name is the name of God incarnate—which means that God made himself into a person and came to be with people as one of them. Of course that makes His name even more special. There is power right now, today, in just saying the name of Jesus over and over.

There is a section in the Gospel of John in the Bible that tells us what Jesus said about asking in His name. He said that if we ask anything in His name, the Father will give it to us. Those words don't make some kind of magic like "abracadabra." Adding "in Jesus' name" to whatever I can think of to ask won't cause me to get it. Still, Jesus meant *something* when He said that. Let's see if we can catch a glimpse of it.

Jesus is the incarnation of God and God is love—not just sentiment or romance, but more like a very hot fire that burns away whatever is less than pure. To be in this kind of hot fire takes away all the self-centered things we want and focuses us on whatever is truly the best for the most people. If we are completely in God's love, there is nothing in us but the kind of perfect caring that He has for each person He created. He has showed us that it is possible to be a fully human person and to experience God's love at the same time. When we see Jesus being both human and all-loving at once, it makes us want to, ourselves.

The best way to identify with the way Jesus *is* is to team up with Him. We can learn from Him and love Him and ask Him to help us grow more like Him. It is a gradual process, of course, just like any growing. If, as you are growing up, you say, "I am in the family of Tom Jones," you are linking yourself to the name of Tom Jones and doing things the way his family does them. If you say, "I am in the family of Jesus Christ," you are linking yourself to Him. You are letting everyone know that you are teamed up with Him and are playing with the other players who are on His team because they are His family. Likewise, you are using His rules. You are doing things His way.

Some people think Jesus' rules are long and complicated and that it is really impossible to play by them. They are not long and complicated at all. He really gave us just one rule: love. His love is the rule; all the others are just subheadings underneath. Jesus told us that when we play on His team with His family and follow His rule, we will have help doing it; the Holy Spirit is ready to help. And as we play, we begin to realize what "in Jesus' name" really means. It means as we grow and change we want to become more and more like Jesus. You've seen families where everybody looked a lot alike; where the family resemblance was so strong you could tell its members before you were introduced, haven't you? What we are doing when we pray is asking for help for ourselves and whoever we pray for to grow to have a true family resemblance to Jesus. He is like the Father, you know, because He is the incarnation of God. When we say "in Jesus' name," we are also saying "as Jesus would pray."

Sometimes prayers are not answered "yes" but are answered "no." Maybe those are the prayers in which we have asked for things that would *not* help us to become more like Jesus. God would certainly not give us anything that wouldn't push us along to the goal of becoming what He wants us to be.

Jesus told us that prayers in His name would for sure be answered. If we pray "in Jesus' name" and we think our prayers are not answered, perhaps we need to check out what we are asking and why. Maybe they are not in Jesus' name at all but instead in our own names. And maybe the reasons we want what we have asked for are not for love or becoming like Jesus, but for selfish or unkind purposes. Sometimes, too, we ask for what seems right to us and it isn't right in God's much bigger, better plan.

Lots of people tack on "in Jesus' name" at the end of a prayer without thinking about it at all. Their words are habit. Even so, it isn't a bad habit to have. Even mentioning His name brings a person a little closer to Jesus' person. And that is the most important thing prayer can ever do for us or those we pray for. Receiving what we want might not matter. But being closer to and more like Jesus matters most of all.

*Yahweh, you examine me and know me, you know if I
am standing or sitting, you read my thoughts from far away,
whether I walk or lie down, you are watching, you know
every detail of my conduct. . . . It was you who created my
inmost self, and put me together in my mother's womb; for
all these mysteries I thank you: for the wonder of myself, for
the wonder of your works.—Psalm 139:1-3, 13-14*

Chapter 19

The One-Way Mirror

Is it wrong to pray so much for myself?

There was a lot of change taking place in Jim's life. He
had found a new way to relate to his mother, which they
were both enjoying. He had made a success as a beginning
debater and had found Mary and Marty, friends his own
age with whom he could share even his new spiritual journey. I didn't see him as often as I had in the fall and winter.
I missed him. So one day in early spring when he called and
asked me if we could talk, I was unashamedly pleased. I
baked a batch of chocolate chip cookies and piled a big
serving of them into my basket. It was still too cold to sit in
the park, so we met in the conversation room at the library.

Jim was growing physically, too, I realized at once. I
could see a lot more wrist below his shirt sleeves than before.

"Well, what's up?" I asked him, opening my basket of
cookies.

His smile was no different. Neither was his enthusiasm
for chocolate chip cookies. But his question was a very mature one—one that I wondered about myself for years. In

fact, I had just barely touched an insight into it when he brought up the question.

"I feel guilty if I pray for myself. But I keep doing it. It seems like I sure have a lot of things just about me; and it's selfish, isn't it? Shouldn't I forget myself and pray for other people?"

Lord, inside myself I feel the answer to Jim's question. How can I make it clear enough for him to understand?

FOR JIM:

Supposing you were in a room that had a window made of the kind of glass through which you can see only one way. And supposing you didn't know the window was there. Then imagine you were tired and cold and had a big splinter under your fingernail. Since you didn't know there was one-way glass in the room, you were crying or swearing or whatever you felt like doing. Supposing you had run the splinter under your nail yourself and were mad at yourself because you had been so stupid and careless as to do a thing like that. So, besides everything else, you were telling yourself how mad you were at your own clumsiness.

Now just to make it complicated, suppose there was someone very special on whom you were trying to make a good impression and, without your knowing it, he was watching you through the glass. A mess, don't you think? Don't you suppose that after you found out the person had been watching and listening to all you had to say, you'd give up trying to impress him anymore?

I'm really not off the subject at all. We sometimes forget that God knows all about us: that we're naked, hurting, mad at ourselves, wishing we could do and be better than we can. He also knows all the good things He put inside us and all of our fine qualities. He knows we would like to be perfect—and He knows when we're not. He can see us just exactly as we are, both inside and outside. Besides that— and more important than anything else—He loves us. He loves each one of us more than we can imagine with our best imaginations. Being naked and angry and hurting and having Someone know about it isn't so bad if we realize that Someone loves us more than we can believe.

Now back to praying for other people: it is almost impossible to pray for or even think about anyone else when we are hurting or afraid or miserable any other way. Maybe some of the famous saints of history have succeeded in turning their pain into perfect prayers for other people; but most of us, if we're honest with ourselves, know that we can't pray very well for someone else while suffering from a long splinter under the fingernail. I am *not* saying that we must just forget everyone else until we feel perfect, though. Not much praying for others would get done if we waited until all conditions were exactly perfect before we began to pray. What I am saying is that each of us needs to realize that God really truly does know everything about us and loves us anyhow. He knows when we want to pray for other people and when we have big bad problems of our own. Because He knows all that, we can go about praying for both ourselves and others in a whole different way.

When Jesus told us to love our neighbors as ourselves, He was saying that we are supposed to love ourselves. You might as well say that unless we know a little about loving ourselves, we aren't ever able to love anybody else. One of the first points about loving ourselves is to feel that we are special enough to God that He will take care of us. I can't put much feeling into asking God to take care of somebody else unless I am aware deep down that He is taking care of me. So the first part of praying for another person is to get rid of all my own needs by giving them over to God to tend to. Sometimes that takes some time. We have to have a little honesty session in which we tell God just exactly how we feel without pretending anything at all. We have to acknowledge that we are having some problems which are keeping us from concentrating on anything anybody else needs. After that, the feelings of peace come over us and we can say honestly that we don't have to worry anymore about ourselves.

Time as we know it isn't important to God. He wants us to keep our eyes on Him—to love Him and to trust Him. If it takes a day or a month or even more for us to give all of our problems and worries over to Him so we can be free of them, He doesn't care. He is patiently caring for you through each part of your growing up just as your parents have been all your life. Part of becoming an adult is being able to turn our own lives over to God and then being free to help and pray for other people.

What you can do is tell God, your Father, just how you feel and ask Him to give you the peace that comes from truly *knowing* He is taking care of you. Then, when that peace comes, you will find yourself praying for other people. Nobody is ever through caring about himself. No matter how old you are, there will be times you will have to stop praying for someone else until your own needs and problems have been given over to God. He loves you, and isn't it good to remember that when you think you should be praying for someone else, He knows that? He knows whom you think you should pray for and why. Don't you suppose He can translate your good intentions into prayers while you are taking care of a splinter under your fingernail? I think so.

He provides for all living creatures, his love is everlasting!
Give thanks to the God of Heaven, his love is everlasting!
—Psalm 136:25-26

Chapter 20

The Robin

IS prayer for the birds?

"Look, that robin's praying." Jim's eyes were dancing with delight. It was a first-of-summer day with golden sunshine and clear, crisp sky.

"I thought he was listening for a worm."

"Well, what's the difference? He was praying for a worm and now he is listening for the answer to his prayer."

I laughed and hugged Jim quickly before the girls saw me.

"Do you remember what you said last fall before we started talking about prayer?" I asked Jim. He shook his head.

"What?"

"You said 'prayer is for the birds.' And then you told me how stuffy it seemed to you. And now you have just said it again: 'A robin is praying. So maybe prayer *is* for the birds and we just didn't realize it."

And then Jim gave me the lecture for the day.

"Well, sure! Inside themselves they expect God to take care of them, so all they do is wait to go get what He gives them. But they have to go after it themselves, 'cause if they didn't, just flying around and around for nothing all day would be awful boring."

Jim had seen the picture. Our lives are to be lived in an attitude of prayer: of cooperation and shared love with a perfect Creator who loves us each as if there were no one else. The robin hears his answer moving in the earth under his feet. Do we hear our own answers as well? The robin flies about, having no worry about the availability of his sky and he knows that the material for his nest is around somewhere within his reach. He has a relationship with his Maker which is not intellectual, but which is nonetheless real. We could do worse than to model our lives after his.

But we can do better, too. The Love which created the robin is alive and approachable. Like Jim, we can question it, relate to it, know it, and enjoy it. We can do so because "it" is *He*! He is our Friend. All winter I had watched Jim's progress, shared his problems, fed his body and his spirit. He had become one of my dearest friends. How much more was the Father who created him enjoying his progress. I saw Jim once in a while. The Father saw him all the time, watched every little newness be born and grow in his spiritual life. Jim was living like the birds: in constant communion with the One who fashioned him before the world was born.

Jim had learned, and I had learned with him, that there are many dimensions of prayer. We scratched the surface in our months of questioning, but we didn't find all the answers. I hope we never do. I like to question and hear the Holy Spirit define the answers. I like to feel the gaps in my understanding of the magnitude of God's love being filled up—with more and more of that love. Prayer is for the birds, Jim. Amen.